More Praise
Stanley and S

"Affectionate . . . Stanley and Sophie are rendered with such warmth and wit."

—*Publishers Weekly*

"Jennings is a wonderfully precise writer. Her punchy, lean prose is one of this book's delights. Ditto her bone-dry wit. *Stanley and Sophie* is studded with evocative, often very funny cameos of Manhattan dog life that you don't have to be a dog person to relish. . . . *Stanley and Sophie* is a moving account of how we love and how we mourn."

—Michelle de Kretser, *The Age* (Australia)

"A real-life account of the dogs that change us. If you're a dog person you'll relate entirely."

—Marjorie Kehe, *The Christian Science Monitor*

"*Stanley and Sophie* sacrifices sweetness for some harsh realities: losing a husband, living in post-9/11 New York, and adopting two dogs in hopes of companionship."

—Newsweek.com

"Has human being ever loved canine companion as fiercely as Kate Jennings loved her border terriers, Stanley and Sophie? With both of them it was love at first sight, their communion igniting on an almost mystical plane. . . . Jennings, a tough New Yorker brought up as a tough Australian, is a crisply pensive stylist . . . a deft sketcher of New York types and a perceptive observer of animals."

—Craig Seligman, Bloomberg

"For border terrier fans and owners, in fact for any dog lovers, this book will be an unmitigated delight . . . sad and delightful, considered and engaging. Kate Jennings is one of our finest writers. . . . Unexpectedly moving."

—Michael Williams, *Australian Book Review*

"Capture[s] quite a few of the traits we all know and love in our own companions . . . laugh-out-loud moments with plenty of introspection and self-examination."

—Ellen Redman, *The Borderline*

"The story of two dogs who helped their owner heal a broken heart."

—*Taconic Press*

"Kate Jennings has brought all her human complexity into her feelings for two border terriers. There's nothing sentimental about this wondrous book—just unsparing truth, a trained eye for detail, and a beautifully clean style. This small book takes us from the East Side of Manhattan to the author's native Australia and on to Bali, but it also ferries us from grief to love to loss and back again to a dual sense of love *and* loss."

—Edmund White, author of *Hotel de Dream: A New York Novel*

"I devoured this book. Kate Jennings has written a frank and eloquent memoir about her most private and public concerns. This is the story of two terriers who inadvertently mend the author's broken heart. They also change the way she views all living creatures. Jennings travels the world making connections between our pampered pets, pariah dogs, and two charming pigtailed macaques rescued from an Indonesian market. Insights into the myriad ways that animals sustain us spill out of this book. Jennings takes no prisoners. She will make you laugh, cry, and run out to get your own dog a big bone."

—Elizabeth Hess, author of *Nim Chimpsky:*
The Chimp Who Would Be Human

"The canine psychodrama between Stanley and Sophie makes Britney and Kevin look calm and well-adjusted. As for Chico and Cheeky, the monkeys in this star-crossed story, they're the Heathcliff and Cathy of Bali. The book itself? Positively Proustian."

—Simon Doonan, author of *Eccentric Glamour:*
Creating an Insanely More Fabulous You

ALSO BY KATE JENNINGS

POETRY

Come to Me, My Melancholy Baby
Mother, I'm Rooted (editor)
Cats, Dogs & Pitchforks

STORIES

Women Falling Down in the Street

NOVELS

Snake
Moral Hazard

ESSAYS

Save Me, Joe Louis
Bad Manners

Stanley
and Sophie

KATE JENNINGS

SCRIBNER

New York London Toronto Sydney

Scribner
A Division of Simon & Schuster, Inc.
1230 Avenue of the Americas
New York, NY 10020

First Scribner trade paperback edition August 2009

SCRIBNER and design are registered trademarks of The Gale Group, Inc., used
under license by Simon & Schuster, Inc., the publisher of this work.

For information about special discounts for bulk purchases, please contact Simon &
Schuster Special Sales at 1-866-506-1949 or business@simonandschuster.com.

The Simon & Schuster Speakers Bureau can bring authors to your live event. For
more information or to book an event contact the Simon & Schuster Speakers
Bureau at 1-866-248-3049 or visit our website at www.simonspeakers.com.

Manufactured in the United States of America

2 4 6 8 10 9 7 5 3 1

Library of Congress Control Number: 2007049808

ISBN: 978-1-4165-6029-6
ISBN: 978-1-4165-6030-2 (pbk)
ISBN: 978-1-4165-6038-8 (ebook)

For
Roberto
where the story began
and for
Irene
Christopher and James
Sigrid and Desmond

I was sore at my whole life.

—Clifford Odets

New York

1.

A Cappella

Joe Cocker, the rock star, was underestimated, even in his heyday. He had the voice of an angel and the appearance of a mental hospital patient. His signature song, unless you count "She Came in Through the Bathroom Window," was the antiphonal Lennon-McCartney tune "With a Little Help from My Friends," which Cocker made his own by using waltz time and incorporating chorics with raw rock, much as the Rolling Stones did in "You Can't Always Get What You Want." My favorite part: Cocker's girl group carols, "Do you need anybody?" and Cocker confesses with distinctly manly candor, "I need someone to love." Then the girls ask, a cappella, "Would you believe in a love at first sight?" and he answers, "I'm certain that it happens all the time." I always shake my head at this. Doubtful. Very doubtful.

I've been insanely, destructively in love several times in my life, the details of which I'd rather not remember. (Neither adverb is an exaggeration; such was my derangement that certain people still walk out of a room when I walk into it. My excuse: I was young; it was the sixties; derangement, courtesy of R. D. Laing, had cachet.) And I was married for many years to a man for whom, I always said, I would walk a crooked mile. But love at first sight? No. The only time I've fallen in love at first sight was with dogs.

The first was Stanley, an aristocratic alpha male border terrier. Best of breed, pure princeling. (Kennel name: Bramble-bee Borage, out of Wizard Notice of Bramblebee and Faithful One of Bramblebee.) The second was Sophie, a streetwise, scrappy, orphaned alpha female, also a border terrier, not to be confused with a border collie, an altogether different kind of dog. In my love for these two dogs lies a tale about human need, the kind that blots out all sense—in this case, the sense of having two rivalrous terriers with more volatility and energy than the ocean in a New York City apartment. Human need—*immense* subject.

And because Stanley came into my life in 2001 and Sophie in 2004, it's a tale, tangentially, about Manhattan in those first confounding, politically charged years of the new millennium. Years when our lives were a rhubarb of noisy emotion: a devil's chorus of fear, blatting rage, birring anxiety, tweedling incredulity, roupy sorrow.

2.

Miniature to Massive

New York is a city of dogs. A vast poochdom. (Eight million people, five million pets, a high proportion of them dogs.) If you were to idle on my street—East Seventy-second—for only a short while, you would witness a cavalcade of dogs, from miniature to massive, in the singular, plural, and excessively plural, dogs in bulk considered not over the top or even eccentric, such as the eight King Charles spaniels, more gaggle than pack, who issue from the building next to mine.

In the early-morning hours, you'd see dog owners dressed for work taking their charges around the block "to do their business," the owners brisk and impatient, the dogs put upon and dawdling. Also abroad are the dedicated dogs-as-a-way-of-life crowd, a social club of sorts, a clique, for they all know one another, conversing with Woody Allen earnestness but rarely, to judge from my interactions with them, his humor. They wear fanny packs and carry water bottles, and their dogs are usually large—boxers, mastiffs, Rhodesian ridgebacks, Afghan hounds, Dobermans, Great Danes—and they're headed toward Central Park, where dogs are allowed the courtesy of being off their leashes before nine A.M. You'd see the nine-to-fivers again in the evening hours, more relaxed, taking deep breaths, snatching moments away from the claustrophobia of domesticity, allowing their dogs to sniff at will, with the heaviest traffic at ten P.M., when prime-time telly finishes, the men among them smoking fragrantly stinky cigars, verboten in the apartment.

Around eleven A.M., the first of the professional dog walkers can be sighted, the boutique kind who take on only one or two dogs at a time and charge a bundle, as well as those who work in pairs with up to ten apiece—urban armadas—one walker to stay with the dogs at street level while the other fetches or delivers a "client" to or from an apartment. You might also spot dogs in the care of maids—those yappy King Charles spaniels are usually shepherded by a particularly unsmiling housekeeper—or off-duty doormen earning a few extra bucks. And then there are those who work from home and can walk their pooches whenever they like. Writers such as me, for example. This last group probably wouldn't see the light of day if not for dogs.

While you will see every breed of dog listed with the American Kennel Club, you won't see many mongrels or, as we call them in my native Australia, "bitsas": bits of this and that. Here, those of us who might be characterized as bleeding-heart liberals are more likely to apply to a breed rescue organization for a dog than to find one at a pound. That way we get to salve our social consciences and have a classy dog at the same time. Indeed, you can tell a lot about New Yorkers from their dogs—as with everything else, we make statements with them, purposefully telegraphing information about our aspirations, status, and, yes, politics through our choice of breed.

Stanley and Sophie

We acquire dogs for a number of reasons, some valid, such as valuing their companionship, and some dubious, such as using them as a fashion accessory, deploying them as pickup bait, or completing a Madison Avenue idea of what constitutes the perfect family. New York City dogs and their owners often resemble each other, much as they do elsewhere in the world, although the effect is heightened when the dogs are dressed like their owners in color-coordinated outfits. My favorite duo in our neighborhood is a woman and her miniature poodle, both coiffed to a fare-thee-well, who, on rainy days, are dressed in shiny white slickers artfully finished with pink kerchiefs around their necks. But the dogs in this town don't just resemble their owners; they act like them. If it's possible for a dog to have attitude, in the sense of a studied, defiant approach to one's environment, then New York City dogs have it in spades.

3.

Boiling, Spitting Oil

Up until Stanley and Sophie, my ideas about dogs were unsentimental and pragmatic, and I was sniffy about people who weren't like-minded. In fact, I worked hard not to succumb to any form of sentimentality. The eighth deadly sin. Babies—I didn't coo over them. The words "cute" and "adorable"— didn't use them. Doggies in the window—walked straight on by. *Little Women*—never read it. Crying in movies—hell no! Call me cold. Actually, call me vinegary. Taking W. C. Fields as a role model was amusing when I was young but had hardened over the years into an unattractive default stance.

I'd grown up on a farm with sheepdogs—dogs with a job. Collies and kelpies, they were treated as workers, housed in kennels made from corrugated iron that were well away from where we lived, near the shearing shed, with no concession to the weather, which in the winter was cold enough for ice to form on puddles and dams and in the summer hot enough to make the lead fall out of pencils. If you were to question these Spartan conditions, my father would tell you deadpan, eyebrows raised a fraction, that it didn't kill them—the dogs were always alive in the morning. A discarded hessian wheat bag on the dirt floor of the kennels: That was permissible. Wouldn't want the dogs turning into sissies. When these dogs grew old and arthritic, they were retired under a rainwater tank where it was blessedly shady, sweetly cool. When their teeth fell out, my father, as did his father, took them to the back of the farm and shot them; you never asked someone else to dispatch them.

We had a yard dog, a bitsa named Bosca, who approached the status of pet, but he also had a job: He cleaned up dinner scraps, patrolled the fence, barked if he saw a snake or heard a car. Sheepdogs never came in the yard, and yard dogs never came in the house, much less curled up in front of the fire or slept on a bed. After all, dogs scavenged carcasses—dead sheep but also hares, kangaroos, possums, goannas, and other wildlife that had met untimely ends—and could have worms. We were all dewormed regularly—livestock, dogs, humans.

I don't remember caring for any of these dogs. No *My Dog Spot* or *Lassie Come Home* story, no child and four-legged friend in my past. The dogs were just there, part of the landscape. My father, though, loved them; they were his comfort in a lonely marriage. They understood him; he understood them. This love wasn't, heaven forbid, expressed, but wherever he went, so went the dogs. My father's undemonstrativeness bothered me until an aunt explained that he had been numbed by the Great Depression. An entire generation of men, she said, dealt with their emotions by bundling them up in a paper bag and placing them out of reach on a high shelf. For the longest time, I thought I would come across that paper bag in the pantry, spotty with grease, shoved away behind preserves, provisions, and kerosene lamps.

Retired now and living in the human equivalent of the space under a rainwater tank, my father has retrieved the paper bag, as I found out when I urged him on the phone from New York to find a dog to keep him company. Our conversation went something like this:

"Dad, do one thing for me. Get a puppy. Or adopt a stray. A dog. Any dog."

"No."

"Why not, Dad? You love dogs."

He turned huffy: "It wouldn't suit my lifestyle."

"And what lifestyle would that be, Dad?" I replied, amused by the idea of my father having a lifestyle. In fact, he does have a lifestyle, and it might even be called alternative: The lonely marriage to my mother ended, to be followed by a loving three-decade-long relationship with another farmer's widow. They spend every weekend and all holidays together, as happy a couple as I've ever seen. When I asked him why they've never married, he said, "I tried that once."

A few months went by, and I broached the subject of a dog again. This time he was even more adamant in his refusal. I threatened to ask someone in his little country town to leave a pup on his doorstep, and then he'd have to take it in. To my enormous surprise, my father started to cry. I could remember times when he was in great distress, but never tears.

"What's wrong, Dad?"

"I had to shoot all my dogs, and I never want to do that again."

I absorbed this remark, the shock of those tears. When conversation takes a serious turn, Australians throw vats of boiling, spitting oil over one another in the form of humor.

They are not denying their emotions; they are obliterating them. "Dad," I said, "I think this time it'll be the other way around. The dog's going to have to shoot you."

Knowing my background, you'll hardly be surprised to learn that I was one of those who thought not only that a dog should have a job but also that keeping them in apartments and always on a leash was close to criminal. People get incensed about confining animals in zoos but are indifferent to being surrounded by dogs that are bred to hunt, herd, guard, or rouse creatures gone to ground reduced to watching pigeons out the windows of apartments while waiting for their owners to come home.

Later, much later, struggling with my dogs' palpable boredom—Stanley crossed his paws in front of him, rested his head on them, and glared; Sophie tucked her legs under her and formed herself into a doleful sausage—and believing it my fault, I mentioned my guilt to my friend Irene, who was a dog walker by trade. Whenever Irene visited—she is one of those empathetic people who can "talk dog"—she was greeted by Stanley and Sophie with such enthusiastic leaping, licking joy that I concluded I must be the worst kind of mother. Short of moving us all to a farm where they could corner foxes, rabbits, and rats, I never seemed able to make them truly happy; scaring the ducks on the Central Park boat pond or disemboweling a stuffed toy didn't quite do it for them. "Don't be silly," Irene said. "*All* my dogs are like that. They're bored out of their brains. That's why they're always over the moon to see me." From then on, I couldn't help but see New York as replete not with man's best friend, frisky and gummily smiling, but reproachful, slouching, neurotic mutts. As a Chinese proverb has it, "The dog that is idle barks at his fleas, but he that is hunting feels them not."

I'm ahead of myself. Over the years, I'd admired other people's dogs; it's hard not to on the streets of New York. I'd had crushes on several breeds—Airedales and boxers—and fantasized about owning one, but the farm girl, or what was left of that girl, always kicked in. I certainly couldn't see myself with a toy breed—sleeve or teacup dogs—those best suited to apartment life; to me they weren't real dogs. Handbags with a heartbeat. And dog ownership in New York City is not just an investment of time but also money, lots of it; vets, grooming, boarding cost a pretty penny. One thing I did know: If ever I had a dog, it would be well trained, like the sheepdogs of my childhood. A whistle, a hand gesture, and they obeyed. Nothing worse than an indulged dog. That, too, was criminal.

4.

Harrods and Hyde Park

I knew about Stanley before he became my baby—my *indulged* baby—because of the nips and scratches a former boss, Roberto, an investment banker, started sporting on his hands and arms. They were inflicted, he told me, by a puppy named after Stanley Holloway, the actor who plays Audrey Hepburn's rascally father in *My Fair Lady*. (For some reason, perhaps their no-frills straightforwardness, border terriers tend to be given upright Victorian names, such as Alfred, Harold, and Ursula, bringing to mind parlors and pudding.)

Stanley wasn't the only one of Roberto's pets to be given a name from *My Fair Lady*. At the time I worked for him as a speechwriter, his New York menagerie included Eliza, Henry, Higgins, and Pickering, all Labradors, and Doolittle, an African Grey parrot who stalked around taking chunks out of unsuspecting Achilles tendons. Roberto was inordinately fond of Doolittle, who mimicked his owner's voice to an uncanny degree. Last but not least, there was Catdog, who came already named. A tiny thing of indeterminate parentage, she had starred in a fashion shoot and was adopted by a model but quickly discarded: Her jet-black coat turned gray in the first rain, the dye puddling beneath her. With a bark in a register that any Cockney flower girl would envy, she had the Labradors cowed.

Stanley spent his puppyhood not in New York but in the care of a housekeeper, Norma, in Roberto's London home, a wedding-cake mansion in Egerton Terrace, a stone's throw from Harrods and Hyde Park. When Stanley was seven months old, Roberto brought him to join the gang in New York. Now, Stanley doesn't like to share; he wants toys and attention to himself. All hell broke loose, I'm told. Stanley beat up the Labs and Catdog and, even less pardonable, jumped into Doolittle's cage and tried to defeather him. He was only being a terrier, of course. I received a panicked phone call from Roberto. Would I take Stanley for the weekend and see if I liked him?

An hour later, Stanley stepped off the elevator on my floor and looked to the left, where I stood waiting. And that was it. *Coup de foudre.* I fell in love with a prideful, tense bundle of muscle and sinew that stood seventeen inches high. You would see a small brown dog; I saw perfection, a handsome, Rhodes Scholar–smart terrier who had velvety black-brown ears folded with origami precision; dark eyes—intense, knowing, rimmed as if with kohl; a grizzle coat—brown mixed with red and gray, with a pleasing rough texture; elegant limousine legs; tail always aloft; a creature alert from his definite muzzle to his dewclaws, a presence that couldn't be ignored. My darling boy.

Some years later, I asked the friend who had been given the task of delivering Stanley to me what I was like in that first year with him. "Well, I hope you don't mind me saying this," she replied, "but you were obsessed." Besotted through and through.

5.

Ashes and Ditchwater

When the heart is hard and parched up, come upon me with a shower of mercy. / When grace is lost from life, come with a burst of song. I can remember quoting these lines of famed Indian poet Rabindranath Tagore in those early days and adding that Stanley was my shower of mercy, my burst of song. Faces went expressionless from embarrassment at this admission, but I wasn't exaggerating. I was free-falling, crazed, because my husband had died the year before from Alzheimer's, and as hard as his illness was—it turned out I walked that crooked mile—I was finding his absence and the absence of the demands the disease had made of me even worse. *Freedom's just another word for nothin' left to lose? / Nothin' ain't worth nothin' but it's free.* I was beset by loneliness. A stupid, caterwauling loneliness.

I'm not the kind of person to have regrets or rail against fate. To be sure, I was missing my husband and our marriage, which had been, perhaps, too insular. I'd loved the man, his warmth, humor, optimism, enthusiasm. He'd flat-out adored me, wholeheartedly encouraged my work, given me perspective. My dismal state of mind, though, had more to do with prolonged exposure to Alzheimer's, one of those diseases that undermine purpose and belief in those who witness it. I hadn't been released from it. Instead, I was trapped in a place where reluctance leached through the walls, nihilism pooled on the floor. I tried caulking the holes with work and antidepressants, but still the insistent seepage, still the sorrow. Ashes and ditchwater.

Understandable, then, how I hurdled with ease my long-held objections to dog ownership. Stanley had a job: to bring me into the sunlight. As for dogs bred for the outdoors being unsuited to apartments, well, we human New Yorkers hardly live an ideal life, either, stacked on top of one another.

6.

Exasperating Little Buggers

Sunlight? I'm attributing more thought to myself than I was capable of at the time, but Stanley was a tonic, no two ways about it. Who can stay sad around a creature so evidently bent on discovery, so palpably pleased to be in this world? And he gave structure to my days. No shirking, no pulling up the covers, no turning my face to the wall. Come rain or shine, around the block and farther, at least four times a day. At night he slept with me, starting the evening curled into a tight comma, by morning monopolizing all the pillows like a grand pasha, me pushed down to the bottom of the bed. He was a comfort, a distraction, a puzzle, a new world.

On one of my first walks with Stanley, I ran into a woman who was the sage of the dogs-as-a-way-of-life crowd. I thought of her as the Poodle Lady because she had three enormous standard poodles. Instead of admiring Stanley, she kept her poodles at a distance and eyed him.

"Your first dog?" she asked.

"Yes," I replied, bursting with pride. God, he was *beautiful*.

"You got a *terrier* for your first dog?" she said, incredulous.

I backed off, speculating rudely about the source of her problem. I didn't understand, but I do now: Terriers are not the easiest of dogs; they require a strong, informed hand. They can be wayward, stubborn, and mutinous while also being loyal, loving, and caring, those last characteristics coming with more subparagraphs and provisional clauses than a government contract. They have all the emotions that humans have and a few more besides. They quiver with intent, thrum with curiosity.

Usually, when I don't understand something I turn to books, but I haven't been able to find anything that explains terriers to me. None of the gifted naturalists who have written about dogs—Konrad Lorenz, Gerald Durrell, Vicki Hearne, Elizabeth Marshall Thomas, Desmond Morris, Temple Grandin, the Coppingers—or the literary giants who've made them a subject—Thomas Mann, J. R. Ackerley, Virginia Woolf, Rudyard Kipling—tackle terriers aside from the occasional reference. It's the kind of knowledge, I've concluded, that's passed down through generations of terrier owners. The rest of us are left to muddle along as best we can; we gravitate toward terriers because they are, for the most part, smallish, smart, lively, and fetching, just the ticket, we assume, for urban life, not knowing what we are taking on. (As a point of interest, Lorenz thought large dogs that don't bounce off ceilings, sleep for long stretches, and need only two walks a day were better suited to living in confined spaces, although I'm not sure the dogs themselves would agree.)

Handbooks on the various breeds abound and cover the basics, but those basics apply to any dog. Often these publications are cut-and-paste jobs, with the claim migrating from book to book that the breed in question will make a perfect pet and a great family dog. The books also read as if written, to quote Randall Jarrell, on a typewriter by a typewriter. Only one book I know of—Verité Reily Collins's *About the Border Terrier*—actually has a chapter titled "Do You Really Want to Own a Border?" While Collins agrees that borders are "the grandest little dogs alive," she knows that they require lengthy walks—five miles a day, Collins tells prospective owners, to get her message across—and are also escapologists without peer; they take off and won't return until their investigations are complete. They are self-assertive, thinking terriers, with everything that implies. I recommend her book, along with Frank Jackson and W. Ronald Irving's *Border Terrier*, written with rare flair and humor and published in the seventies by Foyles of London. These books aside, an explanation of the psychology of the exasperating little buggers still needs to be written.

Let me relate the very worst thing that Stanley has done. We were coming out of Central Park at the East Seventy-second Street entrance after walking around the boat pond. Stanley, being fond of perimeters, always insisted on circumnavigating the pond on the very edge of its coping, even though, to his great embarrassment, he once slipped and fell into the water. I had stopped to talk to one of the homeless men who sit on the benches there in the fine weather. I knew always to keep the leash wrapped double around my wrist and hand, but as I talked, my hand relaxed. Behind us, unnoticed by me but not by Stanley, came a Seeing Eye dog, a yellow Labrador, serenely guiding her master. Stanley can't abide Labs, perhaps because of his experience with Roberto's *My Fair Lady* crew; terriers have the memories of elephants. He made a pretense of paying attention to the homeless man and then, with a backward flip, transformed himself into a furry missile, ripping the leash from my hand. Stanley clamped onto the Lab's neck, the blind man fell down, and my darling boy and the Lab, who retained her composure right through the attack, rolled in an ugly ball toward Fifth Avenue traffic.

An almighty commotion erupted, with everyone in the vicinity leaping to help. Stanley was pulled from the Lab, the blind man righted, profuse apologies made, order restored. My heart, however, took some time to beat normally. On the way home, we had words: "For Chrissakes, Stanley, of all possible creatures in the world, a *Seeing-Eye* dog!" Whenever I related this story, non-terrier people were appalled, almost to the point of telling me to have Stanley put down, while terrier owners laughed in sympathy. They'd all had equally devilish encounters.

7.

Hankering

Borders are the last of the true terriers, by which it's meant that, in appearance and character, they haven't changed much since they emerged in the nineteenth century in the border territory of England as varmint hunters. Rats, rabbits, foxes—anything that goes to ground and needs a terrier (from *terra,* for earth) to rouse it. Dogs bred to be "hard as nails," they are of a size to go into burrows and lairs without getting stuck, while also having legs of a length and strength—the breed standard states that their hindquarters should be racy and their loins strong—to follow a horse all day without tiring, with energy left over for a long walk in the evening. By disposition, they are willing to tackle anything: gutsy, determined in the extreme. Working dogs and companions, not pets.

Border aficionados like their dogs to be tough, unspoiled, unassuming. I was once stopped by a woman who saw none of Stanley's evident handsomeness and abundant good qualities. Instead, she informed me that he looked like a doormat. I put as much scorn in my voice as I could when I inquired whether she had at home a fancy-pants dog, such as a Maltese or a Lhasa apso. These dogs, because they are subject to incessant and elaborate grooming, are referred to as the "trimmed" breeds, a fate that hasn't befallen borders because, to quote Frank Jackson and W. Ronald Irving, the border "is largely in the hands of people who appreciate his workmanlike abilities and appearance and who have no desire to see him turned into a little fop." The distaste for foppery on the part of border owners is shared by their dogs; Stanley won't so much as acknowledge the existence of lapdogs, not even to show contempt.

Because they have never been fashionable or a puppy-mill item, subject to careless and unscrupulous breeding practices, borders are long-lived—twenty-one years in the instance of a Kenyan farm border I learned about from another stranger on the street—with few health problems. However, the emphasis by U.S. dog breeders on appearance and not character is beginning to have its fiendish effect even with them. It takes the form of an overemphasis on a head that looks, as the standard puts it, like an otter—broad in skull, short muzzle, eyes wide apart—not on qualities such as keenness or gameness. The eyes are becoming so far apart and the muzzle so attenuated that the dogs don't so much resemble otters as Jackie Kennedy. Health problems—and foppery—can't be too far behind.

And then there is the vexed matter of tails. Jackson and Irving hold that a border's tail should resemble a tine of a harrow, but as most of us wouldn't have a clue what a tine or a harrow is, they invoke instead a carrot when looked at from above, and this carrot should be carried straight, not curled. Jackson and Irving have much more to say on this entrancing subject, including the danger of being too doctrinaire about whether the tail should be held perpendicular to the back or parallel, concluding that it need only be carried well, with confidence. Stanley carries his carrotlike tail at the perpendicular, and he always carries it well, but I can't say the same for most of the borders exhibiting at the Westminster Kennel Club.

Blunt writing like this will get me into trouble with the dog-show set. Jackson and Irving are adept at the diplomacy of this aggressively competitive, overheated world—Christopher Guest's movie *Best in Show,* if anything, underplayed its monomania—which they deflate with choice English drollery. They also have fun with ratting, an activity to which I've never had occasion to give thought, although Stanley has a tribal memory of it, judging from his reaction to the rats that make their appearance at night in the pavement parterres and around the brownstone stoops of New York's Upper East Side. "There are, we suppose," write Jackson and Irving, "few dogs of any breed that won't kill rats after a fashion, but a good Border will kill them with a zest and flair that almost raises the whole thing to an art." If you have a hankering to go ratting, they advise wearing "Wellington boots, or at least tuck your trousers into your socks. To have a rat take refuge up your trouser leg is an experience that you may feel is not entirely necessary to your well-being."

8.

Prickly, Prideful, Independent

Stanley was born on July 17, 2000. He was seven months old when he stepped over the threshold to my apartment. Safely inside and unleashed, he hurtled around, checking every nook and cranny for Labradors and parrots and any other *My Fair Lady* creatures that might be lurking. That done, he piddled grandly in the middle of my bed.

He was house-trained. Before he came to me, he underwent six weeks of puppy training in London, with a certificate from the Dog Hollow School to prove it. I had only to point at his crate, and he would slink into it, the one circumstance when he looked abject—he was embarrassed occasionally, such as when he fell into the boat pond, but not abject. When instructed, he could sit, put out his paw for a treat, or lie down, all in a manner that indicated he was humoring me in what he regarded as a waste of time. He drew the line at "stay," clearly of the opinion that no self-respecting terrier would stay on one side of the room when something interesting was happening on the other. I taught him to heel; he understood that heeling made our walks easier, that there were times when he couldn't sniff and scent absolutely every last bit of the pavement. Ditto with elevator manners—sit, no jumping.

After that first territorial statement on my bed, he confined "accidents" to cocking his leg against the garbage bin in the kitchen when he was feeling particularly peeved or thwarted. As a puppy, he chewed carpets and furniture, destroyed a book or two, ate shoelaces. The usual. Over time my rugs went from being beige and large to multicolored and small. Tribal rugs with dense, irregular motifs, such as Khamseh and Qashqa'i—perfect. English country-house shabby chic, I discovered, owes a lot to dogs.

All the same, life with Stanley over the next few years was a battle of wills. I suspect that this was always the case, to judge from a letter from Norma, Roberto's London housekeeper: "I hope Stanley is a far more disciplinary young man nowadays." He knew perfectly what I was asking of him, but he chose whether to comply on the basis, or so it seemed, of whether it made sense to him. (That's what's meant when borders are called *thinking* terriers.) If he felt a walk had been too short and the day too fine to go indoors, he planted himself on the pavement, took root, no budging him, short of scooping him up and carrying him. Mahatma Gandhi would have been proud. If I corrected him, Stanley sat firm, ears flattened against his head, studiously avoiding my eyes. I'd try not to get cross, but I'm human. On one memorable day, my exasperation caused a woman to appear out of nowhere, shrieking that I was the kind of person who should never own a dog. I shrieked back that I was the best mother in the world. So it goes on the streets of New York.

It's commonplace to say that dogs want nothing more than to please us, which always makes me laugh because Stanley wanted nothing more than for me to please him. He opened half an eye in the morning to see if the world was to his liking, and if it wasn't, I should make it so. It's also commonplace to say we are the "owners" of dogs; I say it myself. More accurately, Stanley and I owned each other.

I've read all about the importance of establishing yourself as the dominant one in the household, the boss, the master, the leader of the pack, and of allowing a dog to be a dog, not a child or a soul mate, et cetera, et cetera. I've watched Cesar Millan's television show, *The Dog Whisperer*: Be macho! Own the throne! Rules, boundaries, limitations! Exercise, discipline, and then, only then, affection. Excellent advice if you have a rottweiler or one of the small breeds, such as Pekingese, who can be notoriously bloody-minded given half the chance. (Just ask hotelier Leona Helmsley's maids.) Stanley wasn't having any of this—he envisaged more of a collegial situation—so I enrolled him in obedience classes with a well-known New York instructor.

Stanley was all suspicion on the day of his first lesson. Unfortunately, the training floor, an odiferous expanse of Astroturf, was directly above a boarding kennel, and the dogs stowed there could be heard barking throughout the building. Stanley responded in kind. Up stalked the trainer as I was trying ineffectually to soothe my boy.

"I bet he does that all the time at home," said the trainer in the coldest, most judgmental of tones.

"No," I replied, refusing to be withered. "Only when the doorbell rings."

"I find that hard to believe," she responded. Dog trainers,

I discovered, are nearly always martinets, but then again, it's a thankless job, with most students of both species flunking. "*That* dog," she continued, "is going to be the *worst* kind of delinquent." At which point Stanley peed on her leg. This was his first lesson, and his last. We didn't return.

Terriers are often thought to be delinquent when they are only being terriers. Here's playwright David Mamet on the subject: "The terrier needs . . . to hunt small rodents. This is its joy. It loves to ferret out, to dig, to nip. It continues to practice its joyful innate behaviors even in the absence of rodents. Their practice, now, however, has a new name: it is called behavioral difficulties." In short, to make them suitable for city life, you have to train the terrier out of them.

Actually, I lied to the trainer. Stanley also barked when I was on the phone for a time that he judged too long, which was troublesome. If I was busy writing to deadline and he wanted a walk, he didn't bark; he just threw himself at me. True to his terrier nature, once determined about something, he never gave up. To discipline him, I sent him to his crate, rattled a can filled with pennies, thwacked a newspaper in his vicinity, or aimed a rolled-up pair of socks at him with as much consistency as I could muster. Mostly he behaved, but sometimes he didn't. I rationalized his lapses by telling myself that I didn't want to break his spirit. A fawning or fearful dog—not for me.

Stanley, his presence, his moods, his persistence, made him a piece of work. Even my dog-walker friend Irene, who occasionally took him for sleepovers at her apartment in the East Village, said that his moments of stubbornness were beyond her ample powers of persuasion and understanding.

But he was cooped up and always leashed, so I forgave him. After all, I wasn't about to enter him in agility trials; he only needed to fit, more or less, into my life, to be my companion. Unconsciously, I'm sure, I wasn't about to punish him for being what I was myself: prickly, prideful, independent.

9.

How Dare He!

Stanley had been with me for only a few weeks when he vac-
uumed up his food even faster than normal, came back into
the living room, tottered, and keeled over, eyes closed, the tip
of his tongue protruding pinkly through his teeth. Alarm!
Mortal alarm! What to do? I hadn't even found a vet. Not that
a vet could help—he was obviously dead. He looked the same
as a cat I once had put to sleep—insulting euphemism, dead is
dead—right down to the tongue. I got angry. *Enraged.* I picked
Stanley up and shook him, shouting that it had taken my husband seven years to die, and him only one minute! How dare
he! Unwittingly, I did the right thing: The shaking dislodged
the food stuck in his windpipe. A glob of unappetizing mashed
meat shot out of his mouth and plopped on the floor. He
stirred, hoisted himself onto his feet, and attempted to walk,
uncertain, wobbly, alive.

10.

God's in His Heaven

Stanley's imperious nature would have made him insufferable if he hadn't also been a champion worrier. His lordliness was bravado. Whenever I returned home, he always greeted me with a little dance made curvy and tight from unbearable anxiety. I'd pick him up to quiet him, and his heart would be hammering: "You came home! You came home! I thought you'd abandoned me!"

After he'd shaken off his morning *langueurs* by lying on his back and squiggling furiously, Stanley spent most of the day patrolling his world. (He had quite a bit of Offissa Pupp's vigilance in him—George Herriman's Officer Bull Pupp, that is, forever alert to Ignatz Mouse's attempts to brain Krazy Kat with a brick.) First the apartment, its rooms and closets, his stash of toys and rawhide bones, followed by the hallway, a quick detour to sniff at the door of an apartment to see if Katie, a bichon frise, was in residence. (Katie had toys that Stanley coveted.) Elevator, lobby, doormen, streets, stores all got the same treatment. He might as well have had a clipboard to tick off items.

Stanley was a social being, with a network of friends in stores around the neighborhood: David at Lexington Gardens, Kirk at Henry Miller, Barbara and Dennis at Hickey's, Angus at Cove Landing, the gang at Leonard's. Well and good if a treat was waiting for him—dog biscuits, of course, but also, at Hickey's, a tasty vitamin pill, and at Henry Miller, a box of small stuffed bears that Kirk kept especially for Stanley, tossing them in the air and scattering them so he could corral and kill them, ratting instinct revving—but what he was really doing was checking that everything was as it had been the day before, and he could quit worrying: *God's in His heaven— / All's right with the world.*

11.

Dogs Don't Care for Irony

My only sibling, a brother younger by two years, exposed to the same pragmatic, no-nonsense farm childhood as I, visited from Australia and chided me for being anthropomorphic. Dare—a family name that singled him out for hazing at his boarding school, Yanco Agricultural High—thought I had become soft and emotionally squishy, not understanding that part of Stanley's attraction was that I could allow myself to be soft in a way that I never would in any other part of my life. I could be warm and forgiving and even downright motherly. I had belatedly discovered the truth in Bob Dylan's observation, made on his *Theme Time Radio Hour*, that you can't trust a man who doesn't tear up watching *Old Yeller*.

"You attribute too much to Stanley," Dare said. I harrumphed. Three days later, he said, in an offhand way, "Stanley's sulking."

"I'd noticed," I replied. Ha! Who's being anthropomorphic now? I paused for a beat. "So what'd you do?"

My brother's turn to pause before saying, "I kicked him off the bed in the middle of the night."

"Well, what did you expect? Hey, he lives here, not you."

Stanley was in a black mood until Dare left. The minute the door closed after him, Stanley brightened and made a victory lap around the apartment. And then he flopped down on the bed from which he'd been evicted and gave a big theatrical sigh: "Tough work restoring order around here!" No coincidence, but that was how I felt. Some of us use dogs to say what we can't to our nearest and dearest. Ventriloquism, not anthropomorphism. My brother is not above using his four-year-old son as an extension of himself, beaming his approval as his son, little Harry, *his* darling boy, *his* best mate, pokes me in the eye.

What we love most about dogs is that they are transparent, their emotions pure, unmuddied by ambiguity even when torn by conflicting desires. They express themselves with graphic simplicity. As Thomas Mann wrote in *Bashan and I,* an exquisite book about a German shorthaired pointer, "[Dogs] are more unrestrained and primitive, less subject to inhibitions of all kinds, and therefore in a certain sense more human in physical expression of their moods than we are."

Their stone honesty forces us to cut the postmodern nonsense and return their emotions in kind. While they can have a grand sense of humor, dogs don't care for irony. Meta-anything bores them. As for signifiers, a rawhide bone is a rawhide bone is a rawhide bone. And for all their artful use of raised eyebrows, deployed with Kabuki-like finesse, they have a preference for pratfalls over smarty-pants knowingness.

At the Hartsdale Pet Cemetery, the oldest of its kind in the United States, the headstones are carved with inscriptions that bear testament to the unadorned love and uncomplicated gratitude elicited by animals:

Stanley and Sophie

IN LOVING MEMORY OF MY FAITHFUL ERICA
GONE BUT NOT FORGOTTEN
POP

JEFF
MY MAGNIFICENT FRIEND

STUMPY
YOU HAD TO KNOW HIM
1955–1975

FLUFFY
A BRILLIANT AND VALIANT CAT

MISSY TOOHEY
THE DAUGHTER WE ALWAYS WANTED

SNOWFLAKE
SEE YOU LATER, GOOD BOY

At one time I would have thought these headstones the ultimate in human folly.

12.

Pickled Feelings

When his dog's spirit was broken after an illness that confined him for weeks to a cage at the vet's office, Thomas Mann observed that "Bashan . . . 'let his head hang,' or 'had a hang-dog look.' He did actually hang his head—hung it low like some wrack of a worn-out cab-horse." All nationalities use dog behavior and appearance to add color to language: "dog-tired"; "dog-eared"; "dog-leg"; "dog days"; "to lie doggo"; "dog's breakfast"; "putting on the dog"; "dog in a manger"; "doggone"; "barking mad"; "lie down with dogs, get up with fleas"; and so forth. The idiom that became vivid for me in Stanley's company was "Let sleeping dogs lie." I tiptoed around in the morning because once Stanley was awake, the day began in earnest.

Italians say *come un cane in chiesa*: like a dog in church. An unwelcome guest. In 2002, on a cold, snowy, messy Christmas Eve, I took Stanley to church. The occasion: my mother's birthday. My mother, a narcissist of the first order, a woman who vastly preferred men to her own sex and from whom I was estranged my entire adult life, had died earlier that year and—how to put this?—I felt she was hanging around, as discontented in the spirit world as she'd been in the fleshly one. A prayer might help. Because I was brought up in the Church of England, I sought out an Episcopalian church. But Manhattan in bad winter weather is worse than the Hindu Kush; salt is spread rather too liberally on our pavements after blizzards, burning Stanley's paws and causing his legs to spasm and seize. Since he refused to wear not only booties but also a coat, which he regarded as the equivalent of a tutu on a football player, I held him in my arms as I leaped over gutters flooded with slush, navigated waist-high mounds of dirty frozen snow——to find every last church locked tight.

Muttering that dogs weren't the only unwelcome guests, I resorted to knocking on the rectory door of the Church of the Resurrection on East Seventy-fourth Street. The pastor made it clear that he thought my request dubious—prayer in a church? what next?—but showed us into the nave, begrudgingly flicking on a single light. Stanley was instantly alert: This was a place unlike any other. His eyes popped, his nose jitterbugged: incense, dust, furniture polish, rodents, aging bodies, saints, sinners. Instead of saying a prayer, I found myself cursing my mother roundly, an outburst fueled by a lifetime of pickled feelings. In no uncertain terms, I told her to stop lurking. Stanley interrupted his wild sniffing to shift closer to me on the pew. I never felt her presence again.

Colloquialisms aren't always flattering to dogs, and some are downright sinister, as they should be. Past generations would scoff at the cozy modern cliché that there aren't bad dogs, only bad people. Dogs span the same spectrum as humans, from psychopaths to saints, their dispositions formed by nature and nurture, just like us, and to say otherwise is to reduce them to blancmange.

I've had cause to invoke the "black dog" of depression, that lounging, implacable, thick-limbed, yellow-eyed beast. Loathsome cur. And when I'm badly troubled, I always envision "the hounds of hell" coming after me, descendants of Cerberus, "the unspeakable, the unmanageable, the savage, the bronze-barking dog of Hades, fifty-headed, and powerful, and without pity." The priests of the Inquisition were called "the hounds of the Lord"—hounds unleashed afresh on the world. To our everlasting shame, dogs were used to intimidate prisoners at Abu Ghraib. Instruments of torture. When those photographs surfaced, I heard dogs invoked in another way: "I wouldn't treat a dog like that." A thoughtless, if telling, figure of speech.

Nothing to do with dogs, but my father used to say, by way of a greeting, "How's your belly where the pig bit you?" Answer: "All healed up and ready for suckling."

13.

I'll Smell Your Arse,
You Smell Mine

After the Poodle Lady questioned my wisdom about having a terrier as my first dog, Stanley and I continued along East Seventy-second Street across Park and Madison, past dowager prewar apartment blocks and the Lycée Français's bulbous Beaux Arts buildings with knots of squeaking Madelines and svelte *mamans* gathered out front on the sidewalk, to Central Park, where we were set upon by a fearsome roaming Rhodesian ridgeback, a dog bred to hunt lions. "Put your dog on a leash!" I shouted at the dog's owner. "Are you crazy?" she said. Being a New Yorker, I wasted no time in calling the Parks Department to complain. And that was how I found out about the contentious courtesy of allowing dogs off-leash before nine A.M. and after nine P.M.

When it came time to decide whether Stanley should be "fixed"—another pussyfooting euphemism—I asked the advice of the Poodle Lady. "He's feisty. He's brave," she said. "But I've seen small dogs like him torn apart by big dogs in the park.

45

Dogs who aren't altered are the ones attacked." (Presumably this dismemberment took place in the courtesy hours.) I also consulted the head of the Northeast Border Terrier Club, informing her that Stanley was a fine specimen, a good addition to the breeding stock here, and she replied that there were many fine borders in the U.S., I should go ahead, get him fixed. I begged to disagree, of course, there was none finer than Stanley, but I made an appointment with the vet all the same. The operation made no difference to Stanley's personality or his weight, as I'd feared, although he never again sat in a corner swaying, his face distinctly dreamy. The vet had wanted to keep him overnight but called me around six to fetch him. The ruckus he was making was deafening: "Ma, get me *out* of here."

Notwithstanding my fleeting fancy of Stanley as a sire, breeding—of any variety—isn't my cup of tea, though it consumed J. R. Ackerley. His book *My Dog Tulip,* a classic of its kind, is the story of a love affair with a German shepherd bitch—a story so intense and downright weird that it makes my obsession with Stanley seem piffling. Tulip's real name was Queenie, but the name was changed to avoid titters because Ackerley, the editor of *The Listener*'s literary supplement, was homosexual. Queenie was not so much a child to Ackerley as a wife, and he the all-forgiving, uxorious husband obsessed with her gynecological functions. Ackerley meant to shock people; he wanted to put "the beastliness back into the beast." This ditty gives an idea of Ackerley's snook-cocking:

> *Piddle piddle seal and sign*
> *I'll smell your arse, you smell mine;*

Stanley and Sophie

Human beings are prudes and bores,
You smell my arse, I'll smell yours.

Peter Parker, in his amusing, affectionate biography of Ackerley, writes that friends found the pair an ordeal because Ackerley blithely allowed Queenie to bite, soil, and chew when the urge took her. He was told by a vet that "dogs aren't difficult to understand. One has to put oneself in their position," advice he took to heart. I must say, it gave me pause to read about someone who crossed the line from besotted to batty. Then again, in a world where excess—except in regard to yoga, interior decoration, and making money—is frowned upon, long live battiness.

When Roberto gave Stanley to me, he intimated that he wasn't a fan of having dogs emasculated—few men are, I've noticed—so I had avoided telling him about Stanley's operation. Out of the blue, he called to say that he was thinking of acquiring a girl border to mate with Stanley. *Uh-oh.* What to do? Find a border that resembled Stanley and had his balls intact? Attach a pair of false balls? Declare Stanley gay? A perfect plot for an episode of Larry David's *Curb Your Enthusiasm.* I eventually told Roberto the truth, and he graciously let the matter slip.

14.

Muck

Thomas Mann fretted about his dog's circumscribed world. Pointers are hunting dogs, but Bashan's life revolved around waiting for Mann to stop work and take him for a sedate stroll in the woods. A red-letter day: The two of them came across a man shooting ducks, to Bashan's bounding delight. When it was time to return home, Bashan was reluctant to leave the hunter and lagged behind Mann instead of cantering in front. This made Mann laugh, but then Bashan committed an unpardonable sin: He began to yawn. "It was this shameless, wide-angle, rudely bored yawning, accompanied by a little piping guttural sound which clearly said: 'My God! talk about a master! Why, he isn't a master at all. He's simply rotten!' " Mann fulminated with comic bitterness and Prussian snobbery about his dog's treachery, telling him to leave and join the man with the "thunder-club": "He does not appear to own a dog, and so he might give you a job. . . . He is, of course, only a plain man in corduroys and no particular class, but in your eyes, no doubt, he is the finest gentleman in the world—a real master for you."

Bashan and I is a luminous book, written during the carnage of World War I. Mann wanted a break from the big subjects, from humans and their sullying ways, and set himself the task of writing "a prose idyll." I understand Mann's impulse. The same scummy soup of geopolitical and mercantile imperatives is again boiling over, giving off a sulfurous stink, leaving us knee-deep in muck. More and more, I hear people say that this is one of those times in history when we can only trust. That sense will prevail? Small hope. I have gone in the other direction, distrusting everyone and everything. *I have seen the future, brother, and it is murder.*

Early on the morning of September 11, 2001, I walked Stanley over to Central Park, our usual route, around the boat pond, to Bethesda Fountain, where you always see, season in, season out, Chinese brides in ratty rented satin, a seemingly inexhaustible supply, like seeding dandelions, bowling along paths and posing in front of water, under willows, against carved balustrades, lifting their skirts to reveal, particularly in cold weather, frayed jeans and scuffed sneakers. For a few hours, a little green, a little grandeur, in their young lives. You also see fashion shoots. In particular, I remember a model in a sleeveless dress, twitching at a photographer, her lipstick luscious against a solemn gray sky, an Irish wolfhound standing next to her, a match to her elongated frame. Reduced to an accessory in silliness, this royal creature pressed his flat ears even flatter against his skull, as dogs sometimes do when they are uncomfortable. On September 11, 2001, the sky was blue. Memorably, famously blue, one of those New York days when you can think of no better place to live.

Back home, Stanley settled to chewing a rawhide bone and I to work. As is my habit, I switched on the television—my electronic hearth—to find that a plane had flown into one of the Twin Towers. All through that day, ash-covered people, their faces emptied of expression from shock, their gaits jerky, filed along the streets, walking long miles home to their apartments. Jet fighters patrolled, helicopters thudded. Wind carried the stench of destruction in our direction. Uptown was order, downtown was chaos. Indelible images, ineradicable fear and sorrow.

15.

Chutzpah

Humans being humans, the emotions of 9/11 were quickly appropriated for purposes that were less than pure. "Terrorism. That's a horse we can ride all the way to the next election," declared Bush strategist Karl Rove. The Republican leadership did exactly that, including, in 2004, goading the nag into New York City for their convention. Normally Republican politicians convey the impression that they wouldn't mind if New York, home to just about everything they despise, dropped into the sea, FOX headquarters excepted, but the symbolism of holding their convention in the place where the Twin Towers once stood couldn't be passed up.

New York is a moody city, transmitting emotions as if it were an organic being. The week of the convention, the city was unsettled, cautious, as if it couldn't make up its mind how to behave. New Yorkers are especially good at two things: accommodating differences and admiring chutzpah. For the week of the convention, those impulses were at war with the feeling that we were being used and co-opted beyond the bounds of decency, beyond fair play. Insult to injury.

Some residents left town, and the rest of us got on with our lives the best we could, given that closing down even a small chunk of the city causes widespread chaos. I attended the convention as a member of the press. What I remember vividly was not the events inside Madison Square Garden but the atmosphere outside, the buffer zone, where whole blocks of buildings and streets were cleared of people and cars and lit by klieg lights that banished shadows, blanched the walls and pavements, tinged the air white. Even sound was absorbed, as if someone had pressed the mute button. I felt as if I were walking through an overexposed photograph. At Madison Square Garden, shoulder-to-shoulder police formed narrow passageways through which we had to pass; at the edges of the buffer zone, they lined up behind barriers to face demonstrators, trying to look stolid but as uneasy as the rest of us. I couldn't wait to return to my apartment, to Stanley and his curvy dance: "I thought you'd abandoned me!"

16.

Hopeless, Hungry

During the Republican National Convention, someone had the bright idea to hold an auction of Johnny Cash memorabilia at Sotheby's for the delectation of the Texan delegation. Now, anyone who listens to country music knows that Johnny Cash— the Man in Black—was a man of the people, not the plutocrats; he wanted fewer prisons, not more: *I wear the black for the poor and beaten down, / Livin' in the hopeless, hungry side of town.* Protestors jumped on the event. As Sotheby's is on East Seventy-second Street, over near the East River, I couldn't resist walking Stanley in that direction around the time a demonstration was planned.

We found a ragtag group of demonstrators assembled on the pavement opposite Sotheby's, behind a large homemade banner on which was scrawled SEND W. TO FOLSOM, referring to the correctional facility that inspired Cash's "Folsom Prison Blues." Other placards declared sentiments such as I WALK THE LINE FOR JOHN KERRY. While we waited for the Texan delegation, we warbled and yowled Johnny Cash songs. No one could carry a tune. Delighted at the silly rowdiness, Stanley joined in, yipping as if born on the range.

A bus pulled up in front of Sotheby's, and the Texan delegation, wearing their trademark white Stetsons, cream sport coats, checked shirts, and bolos, poured onto the sidewalk. Men in white vying to buy a piece of the Man in Black. Someone was getting things badly wrong, if not completely arse-backward. Police expertly shuffled the conventioneers into the lobby, but not before they saw—and heard—us. Heads jerked back in puzzlement; some burst out laughing. We didn't mind; this was vintage New York fun.

The Man in Black wouldn't have minded, either. Cash could be a regular cutup. Witness a track on his Folsom Prison concert album, titled "Dirty Old Egg-Suckin' Dog":

> Well he's not very handsome to look at
> Oh he's shaggy and he eats like a hog
> And he's always killin' my chickens
> That dirty old egg-suckin' dog
>
> Now if he don't stop eatin' my eggs up
> Though I'm not a real bad guy
> I'm gonna get my rifle and send him
> To that great chicken house in the sky

He sang it in the lachrymose, syrupy style made famous by Red Foley—*When I was a lad and Old Shep was a pup / Over hills and meadows we'd stray*—which set the inmates to cackling and whistling. He followed it up with "Flushed from the Bathroom of Your Heart," which had 'em in the aisles.

Singing Johnny Cash songs was an improvement over singing "God Bless America," which became obligatory and oppressive in the months after 9/11. No matter the event, it was sung—America keeping its pecker up. As an antidote, my friends and I made up alternative words: *God bless Stanley, dog that I love / Stand beside me and guide me / As I scoop the poop from above / From East Seventy-second Street / To the Hamptons . . .* Hey, it helped. I wasn't the only one having trouble with blind patriotism. Without humor, we're doomed. Maybe doomed anyway.

On the way home from the Johnny Cash demonstration, I sat on a stoop, Stanley at my feet, and watched a grand piano being hoisted twenty stories into an apartment. This operation was simplicity itself and satisfyingly ages old, never improved on through history: a winch on the roof, two men on the ground with ropes to guide the piano and keep it from swinging wildly and bashing into the building. A brisk breeze added a little drama. Men were posted to stop passersby from walking directly under the piano. This is one of the oddities of New York that never ceases to amaze me: People simply don't notice what's going on above them, in this case a grand piano hovering only yards from their heads, like a silent-movie gag. It was not hard to imagine the stone-faced ghost of Buster Keaton somewhere near, having an inward chuckle.

17.

Deliciousness

Dogs need other dogs, and Stanley was no exception. Some he liked, some he didn't, and one he loved, a big schlumpy golden retriever named Alice. She was his companion at a house at Sagaponack, on Long Island, where we often stayed. Stanley understood immediately that Alice, the sweetest and most patient of creatures, was his host, and she understood that he was a young punk with a big heart. They were good for each other: She needed exercise, and Stanley provided that, urging her to be up and about. For his part, he needed to be taught manners, a task she undertook with forgiving patience.

I had some of the most contented moments of my life sitting on the back steps of the house and watching Alice and Stanley roughhousing on the lush green lawn as the sun went down, the day cooled, the shadows deepened. Wrestling, rolling, chasing, grunting, snorting, mouthing. Stanley would thread himself between Alice's legs as if he were a croquet ball and she were a wicket, or he would grab hold of her neck with his teeth and make her take him for a ride. Alice could put Stanley's entire head in her mouth. When they grew tired, they sat companionably side by side until their panting subsided, and then Stanley licked Alice clean of drool. Sometimes they got their second wind; this was a game with infinite variations and no time limit. Sometimes he went too far, and she boxed his ears and sloped off to her favorite snoozing spot under a bush.

Alice never wandered, but I learned the hard way, my heart in my throat, to keep Stanley always tethered or on a leash. He could clear a high fence and be a speck on the horizon before you could say Bramblebee Borage. He was more than fleet: Now you see him, now you don't. His prodigious leaping, his ability to go from stock-still to a hundred miles per hour—nothing in between—and his dexterity with a basketball, a favorite toy that he dribbled furiously all around the apartment, made me give him a middle name: Sprewell. (This, back when the New York Knicks were a professional basketball team and not a bunch of spoiled, monumentally inept, badly managed losers, before Latrell Sprewell was traded to the Timberwolves.) The problem was that Stanley could appear to be content with our routine when in fact he was plotting and planning the perfect moment to make a prison break. He had places to go, some of them across roads, and he never looked both ways to see if cars were coming; no border does, and being small and brown and barely visible from the vantage point of a steering wheel, many of them meet their end in the street.

Sagaponack beach in the winter: not a soul in sight, wind raking the sand, sullen waves crumping on the shore, sea and sky glazed green-gray. Lost in thought, I had walked some distance, the leash dragging behind me, before I realized Stanley wasn't attached. He hadn't made a rush for freedom into the dune grass or rosa rugosa thickets but instead was trotting along beside the leash, regarding me somewhat scornfully but also with concern: "Ma, you've got it wrong! *Again!* I'm supposed to be on the end of that thing." All was not right in his world.

Each night, Alice at my feet, Stanley next to me, we watched television while I brushed them and inspected for ticks. The antitick medication, Frontline, easily applied through skin on the nape of the neck, works well, but with Lyme disease as a possibility, one can never be too careful. First their topside, then their tummies. Oh my God, what is *that*?! Attached to the tip of Stanley's penis—okay, yes, I referred to it as his pee-pee—was a round glaucous blob. An engorged tick? It was too late to call a vet. I put Stanley on a table and, with a pair of tweezers, nervously tried to extract the tick. Instead of coming off, the blob stretched. And stretched some more. It was gum.

When Stanley chewed a hole in an antique kilim at the Sagaponack house, my response was to ask my host—the human one—whether she was sure he was the culprit and then to point out, ever so helpfully, that it was a neat hole. On my next visit, she reminded me to keep a close watch on Stanley. As I was vehemently defending him and thinking her a fusspot, I glanced down: Stanley was watching us, head tilted in studied innocence, a tiny thread of red kilim protruding from the side of his mouth. Trying not to giggle, I diverted her attention. I'd joined J. R. Ackerley: batty as all hell when it came to my dog.

This I remember: Stanley stretched out on the grass on the

back lawn, his tether at its limit, taking it all in, catching every smell and sound, absorbed, fulfilled. Back in the city, he'd conk out, sleep for a day straight, and wake up with a wistful expression: "Where'd all the deliciousness go?"

18.

Bad Idea

Stanley and I had finished greeting Massoud, the fruit vendor on the corner of Seventy-second and Lexington Avenue, a fellow who hates the cold and at the smallest cloud disappears for days. We were passing in front of Swifty's, a socialite watering hole, when we were stopped by a young man. I'd seen him around; he was a dog walker. "Is that what a border is supposed to look like?" he asked, referring to Stanley's crisp, articulated, recently groomed coat. I replied in the affirmative and explained that Stanley was hand-stripped, a method whereby the wiry outer coat is pulled out between thumb and forefinger when it's "blown," as show people call it—that is, shaggy and shedding—while preserving the soft undercoat. Mechanical clipping destroys the outer coat, which evolved to provide protection in bad weather. A border's pelt should be rough to the touch, like sturdy tweed cloth, and lie close to the body. The dog walker introduced himself—Paulo—and told me that he had on his hands a two-year-old female border whose owner had died. "Call me if you want a home for her," I said, giving him my number.

Stanley was stripped by Kris, a nuggety, sardonic fellow who goes from apartment to apartment tending to Upper East Side terriers. Dog strippers are few and far between; I know of only one other expert dog stripper in Manhattan, and that's kindly Richard, whom I sometimes used. Richard was trained by Kris and works in the basement of a Chelsea row house over on Ninth Avenue. It's a specialized trade, hard on the wrists and requiring a fastidious nature, not to mention an ability to "talk dog." Stanley submitted to the process with ill grace, but he thought better of getting on Kris's wrong side, which would earn him a sharp belt on the nose. Afterward, spruced up and knowing it, Stanley would canter around the apartment as if he were a show pony; my boy had a touch of vanity. Putting on the dog.

Having worked in kennels since he was fifteen, Kris was a fund of gossip about the dog-show world, which has something in common with baseball: Stars of Westminster are occasionally helped along by artificial means, specifically Clairol and boot polish, despite a ban on this kind of enhancement. And these stars don't necessarily have nice temperaments. In fact, while splendidly handsome, they can be downright mean. Appearance over character.

What little I'd learned about terriers came from Kris, who started grooming Stanley soon after Roberto gave him to me. Every three months, Kris set up his gear on the kitchen countertop, and I'd stand nearby and pepper him with questions. Kris had as many reservations about Stanley and my ability to handle him as the snippy dog trainer, but when Stanley entered full adulthood—three years old—Kris allowed that Stanley hadn't turned out as badly as he'd assumed, at least not in comparison with some of his other charges; I hid my pleased smirk. So it was Kris I consulted after my encounter with Paulo. Stanley's boredom was weighing heavily on me; another dog would keep him occupied. I was busy conjuring up images of two borders gamboling through the day and sleeping spooned together at night. "Don't," said Kris. "*Bad* idea. You have no idea of the work or problems involved."

19.

Handstand

I pushed the idea of another dog out of my mind. Three months later the phone rang. On the other end was Paulo. "The dog walker," he reminded me. He told me that if I wanted Sophie, I could collect her. They were outside on the corner of Third Avenue and Seventy-third Street. Without hesitation, I was out the door, up the street, giddy with apprehension and expectation.

Paulo was holding Sophie in his arms. She looked up at me, and it happened again: *Bouleversée*. Besotted. *Brothers and sisters, I bid you beware / Of giving your heart to a dog to tear.*

Sophie wasn't best of breed. She had short legs and a bent tail that was never at the perpendicular. She hippity-hopped along rather than ran. And because her coat, reddish-blond in color, had been clipped mechanically rather than stripped by hand, it was thin and unruly; she always looked somewhat dishabille—Marilyn Monroe–ish. But she made up for her faults with an angelic face and, underneath, a steely orphan-girl determination.

She was different from Stanley in one important way:

67

Stanley had no guile; she was all guile. Somehow in her short life, she had learned to assess situations and wait patiently to turn them to her advantage. On arriving in the apartment, she took stock and formulated her guiding principle: "By golly, I've got a new mum, and I'm not going to let any little boy dog get in my way." Sophie's thoughts were, if anything, clearer than Stanley's; I could read them as if they were in a cartoon balloon issuing from her head. When she was disciplined, she'd make a big show of ignoring me for a while, and then, in one of her moments of irrepressible joy, she'd forget and come scooting over, only to screech to a halt: "Whoops, I'm not supposed to be talking to you."

Stanley wasn't pleased. In fact, his nose was bent sideways. He growled when she approached his bed in the study, so I made up one for her on the other side of the room. Stanley proceeded to scuttle between the two; he'd plop down on one and then up and over and plop down on the other. I added a third bed, and he repeated this madness with three bases to cover. Sophie gave up the idea of a bed of her own and retired to the sofa, but when Stanley's back was turned, she went into the study, lickety-split, where she curled up tight as a hibernating dormouse, her head invisible, in the middle of his bed. (Borders are elastic. They can sleep in a ball that's about eight inches across and also sprawl on the floor, legs behind them like a frog, until they reach a length of over three feet.) Stanley stood over her and gave a little uncertain bark, nonplussed that someone would challenge him. He tentatively poked her with a paw. Then harder. He might as well have been trying to force open a sea anemone, fronds clamped against all comers.

The same thing happened with toys, which he wasn't

about to share under any circumstance, not even the tiniest strip of rawhide. Sophie solved that by sneaking out of bed in the middle of the night and having a quiet chew in the dark. In time she developed her own gambits, a favorite being to bop Stanley on the nose and then squeal as if *he* had hit her. Stanley would look at me in dismay: "What's she playing at, Ma? I didn't do it!" She'd purse her features in disdain: "Pussy."

Every day was the same, each trying to trump the other. While Sophie wanted to be loved, she couldn't let Stanley get away with his posturing and prerogatives. If she had just been a tad more submissive and he a tad less overbearing, everything would have been fine rather than a roller coaster of high drama and hurt feelings. The dynamic—part gender, part sibling— was familiar: I'd lived it over and over. I'd find myself thinking, How on earth did this happen? How did it come about that I was spending my days adjudicating between two dogs who were acting out the story of my life?

The story of my life—the story of many strong women of my feminist generation. Just as we copied men, Sophie copied Stanley in every way she could. Stanley only occasionally took a dislike to other dogs, but when he did, it was vehement. Sophie watched him turn hostile and promptly gave it her own twist, taking every opportunity to prove her toughness by going through tail-wagging motions of friendship with some hapless pooch and, just as the other dog was lulled into rubbing noses and sniffing bottoms, turning into a dragon, rearing up, breathing fire. Apologies from me as the disgusted owner pulled the dog away, a quick sideways look from Sophie at Stanley: "See, I can beat up other dogs, too." Napoleons, both of them. Gangstas.

Of all possible behaviors, Sophie also insisted on peeing like him. First she tried lifting her leg in standard boy-dog fashion but lost her balance, which forced her to devise another maneuver, a kind of handstand, front paws on the ground, bottom jacked in the air as high as she could hoist it, the better to cover his mark. Performed with utmost seriousness. And that's how we made our way down the street, Stanley cocking his leg, Sophie doing her handstand, and me trying not to laugh.

Like Stanley, she could fret. Her anxiety manifested itself in vigorous, obsessive licking—she had a tongue as voluminous as Mick Jagger's—to the point where she made holes; she'd start licking and couldn't stop. She had good taste: A cashmere blanket, a Louis Vuitton duffel bag, a George Smith sofa, all developed gaping holes. Much worse, she licked her own leg clean of hair until it was raw, which she did in secret, I discovered, while curled in those tight balls.

Her leg required visits to the vet, as did a urinary infection and a chronically upset tummy. She wasn't house-trained. Although she badly wanted to do the right thing, she'd hippity-hop in excitement after Stanley and forget herself and pee and poop. The joys of dog ownership. She also had the scavenging habits of an orphan, scouring the kitchen for every last crumb and never walking straight on the sidewalk but, rather, weaving along, scoping for food. Slowly, over the period of a year, she learned control. Slowly, her leg healed. Slowly, she was returned to digestive health and knew the joy of a full stomach. The only vestige of her old life was an attraction to motorbikes. She'd hear one gunning curbside and tug hard at the leash, busting to check it out: Paulo had a motorbike.

20.

If I Could Stop the Wind
Blowing, I Would

If I had been doubtful about pack behavior before, I certainly wasn't after watching Stanley and Sophie in action. At home, they noisily acted out their rivalry—sound and fury against cunning—but outside, they joined forces and become a gang of two bent on rumbling the neighborhood.

They divvied up the dog population. Stanley took on the large dogs and Sophie the small. Oh, Sophie, you fooled many an unsuspecting Chihuahua, Pekingese, shih tzu, and toy poodle. Stanley missed saying hello to his old friends, but hey, what can a boy do? Dog owners in the neighborhood now crossed the street when they saw us coming.

I decided that I had to instill some real discipline. The two of them were to walk next to me, at heel, not veer off at whim, acting like the wayward front and back ends of a vaudeville pantomime horse. Any infraction and we stopped, and they had to sit until they regained their composure.

Dog ownership gives New Yorkers a reason to loiter rather

than to hurry—to appreciate, in the case of my Upper East Side neighborhood, a mélange of brownstones, carriage houses, and low and high apartment buildings, the spanking-new and tilting old and everything in between. In New York, bricks and mortar seem almost alive, a composting midden of the city's eras, architectural conversations galore. Dog ownership also gives us a cover to stare unabashedly through windows, especially at night, and imagine the lives within, to approve or censor decorating intent. The art seen this way can be particularly rewarding: Is that a Moore, a Lichtenstein, a Basquiat?

Loitering was what I was doing one evening, checking out some low, wide Federal houses while the dogs sniffed. We'd passed a popular Italian restaurant when we came to a Federal house painted a cheery pink with black trim and a front door that abutted the pavement. At that moment Sophie decided to fly at a miniature Cairn terrier. I'd gotten over my prejudice about toy breeds and become partial to these tiny, bright-eyed, energetic creatures. The novelist Amy Tan, I'm told, has two whom she carries in a bag everywhere she goes. The breed has one problem: Along with being diminutive, they are fragile, with bones that break easily. I'm a little absentminded, and I'd be sure to step on one. After Sophie's outburst, the owner of the Cairn glared and hurried on, and we three stopped while I bent over Sophie, making her sit and think about what she'd just done.

Out of nowhere—in retrospect, he had probably been bending an elbow at the bar in the restaurant—a man appeared, looming over us. Gray suit, yellow tie, tortoiseshell glasses, burgherlike corpulence. A lawyer for sure.

"Your dog is pissing on my door! How dare you allow that

to happen!" His face was mottled with red, and a glob of spittle landed on my surprised upturned face. I looked behind me. Stanley was sniffing at the man's front door.

"He's only sniffing," I said, standing upright. We were nose to nose. "He hasn't done anything."

The man, arms akimbo, launched into a tirade about the unsanitary habits of dogs and their irresponsible owners. I think he might even have quoted John Sparrow, a curmudgeonly Oxford don who famously sneered, "The indefatigable and unsavory engine of pollution—the dog." After that literate beginning, our aggressor descended into expletives. I interrupted to inform him again that my dog wasn't guilty of anything. Then I made the mistake of trying to be reasonable. "Look," I said, "three thousand dogs must pass your door every day on their way to and from Central Park. To stop them from peeing on it would be like asking the wind to stop blowing." Three thousand was an exaggeration; more like one thousand.

"If I could stop the wind blowing, I would!" he bellowed.

I stepped out of spittle range. "Oh." Pause. "You *have* to be a Republican." This was just after George W. Bush was reelected in 2004 with what he regarded as a mandate to steamroll the Constitution. A bitter time. A nation divided. Split by a cleaver.

"Of course I'm a Republican!"

I walked the dogs over to the nearest lamppost and turned to ask the man, "Is this okay with you?"

"We'll see!"

With a little distance between us, I felt emboldened. "You know, I'd hate to be you. I'd hate to know what passes through your mind every night as you go to sleep."

That did it. He roared and pawed the ground, and the

dogs and I beat a hasty retreat down the street. We were almost at the end of the block when I looked back. The man was still there! Still ranting and raving! I did the only thing a reasonable person could do: I gave him the finger.

From then on, whenever we passed his door, I encouraged the dogs to pee on it. (What can I say? Feelings were raw that year.) Stanley always refused—a Republican front door was beneath him. But Sophie obliged. She'd hoist her bottom high in the air and splash her message on the glossy black paint and then look at me for approval.

"*Good* girl, darling Sophie. *Best* girl in the world."

21.

A Crown Jewel

In the hope of putting an end to their gangster routine, I began sending Stanley and Sophie out with the K9 dog-walking outfit, the people who work in pairs and have those small armadas of dogs sorted according to size. The first day I was as nervous as a mother sending a child off to kindergarten. I insisted on accompanying them to the lobby, waving as they disappeared down the street. When they returned, I asked the dog walker—a gentle Brazilian boy—how it had gone. "No problems at all," he answered, and then, cracking a big grin, said, "Um, have you noticed the way Sophie, um . . ." I helped him out: "Have I noticed the way she pees?" He said he'd seen this only once before—in a female bulldog.

My anxiety was unnecessary: The K9 people genuinely love dogs and take excellent care of their charges. As for Stanley and Sophie, they loved their walks, coming back invigorated, giving off the sharp, humid odor that's distinctive to their breed. (One young man in the neighborhood who'd had borders in his family always greeted Stanley by burying his nose in the dog's coat and inhaling deeply: "Ah, that border smell!") It's axiomatic with borders that the more exercise they get, the more they want. I would sometimes come across my dogs on these walks and watch them. Sophie would be in the front group, Stanley in the back, with Sophie checking over her shoulder every minute or so to make sure that Stanley was there.

To give Stanley and me a break from each other, Irene had fallen into the habit of taking him down to her East Village apartment for weekends. He loved these mini-vacations because she carted him along wherever she went, to concerts, parties, street fairs, and art openings, tucked under her arm in a Sherpa carry bag. (To Stanley, Irene meant adventure. She was his Aunt Augusta, the daffy, zesty heroine of the Graham Greene novel *Travels with My Aunt*.) On his first sleepover at Irene's after Sophie's arrival, she was astounded to discover that the toys, for a day or two, were all hers: "Are you sure, Ma?" Her bewilderment turned to ecstasy, and she trundled around the house giving little yips of enjoyment, chewing on rawhide bones and pushing the larger toys with her nose. And then I heard a noise like a miniature foghorn. Sophie was barking while she had a green plastic ball—the flashing variety—in her mouth: *wufflewufflewuffle*. She became inseparable from the ball, playing with it for hours at a stretch.

I expected fireworks over the toys when Stanley came home, but instead he magnanimously allowed her to keep the ball. Nothing else, just the ball. From then on, the first thing Sophie did in the morning was locate the ball and parade it around. If a visitor came, a gala wuffling performance. My orphan girl had a possession, something to count as her very own, as valuable as a crown jewel. She was a woman of means.

It wasn't all tempests and squalls. They roughhoused noisily for hours, skidding in and out of rooms, stopping to get their breath, panting to cool their engines, starting up again. (My neighbors were all dog lovers, which was just as well given the din the two could make.) They even had moments of affection. One of Stanley's ears developed a persistent infection that bothered him no end. I looked up from my work to see Sophie giving his sore ear a vigorous licking inside and out. He responded by putting out a paw and patting her on the cheek. She licked some more, and he patted her again.

22.

You, the Beloved

Irene is a Greek Australian with striking Levantine good looks. She has spent, as she puts it, "nine years on the other end of the leash," grueling years, tough on knees and wrists. One ferocious winter—she'd bought a tiny butane hand-warmer contraption to put inside her gloves and, alarmingly, nearly set fire to herself—I urged her to give it up, to come in out of the elements, and she set about explaining her abiding attachment to her charges:

> I am in awe of how distinct every dog is. They all have strange and endearing qualities. Vulnerabilities that melt your heart or sensitivities that border on the paranormal. Some are so passionate—throaty vocalizing, body vibrating, barely containing their gratitude. And I know it's not food they're after, although it is highly desirable—it's you. You, the Beloved. They forget or simply don't care that you have not loved them as perfectly as they love you.
>
> The years pass and you get to know each one intimately. It's easy. After all, nothing is hidden. They show

79

you everything—joy, silliness, greed, frustration, sadness. And every dog is different. Every single one. How can it be? But what an array of characters! Charlie is so sweet he disarms the most aggressive dog. Zie is so sentimental he almost cries when he sees me. Roxy loves only children and will flop belly-up on the pavement in their path till she gets the child to pet her. Peewee climbs my body like a tree to plant a million licks on my face. Brady is shy and quiet as he approaches me looking for affection.

They all have traits that I struggle with, be it pulling with all their 115-pound heft to get to a dried-up chicken bone in the middle of the main street or mounting their best friend obsessively or waking me at four in the morning with a heavy, nailed paw dragged across my cheek so I can get breakfast. Nobody is perfect, none of us—we're in this together. And they know it.

23.

Bristles and Ribs
and Bony Haunches

An ordinary evening. Walked the dogs around ten, watched Jon Stewart's *The Daily Show* at eleven. Mess O' Potamia, heh, heh. Drifting off to sleep. Low growlings. Both dogs were wide awake in the dark, eyeing each other across the blockade of my body, rumbling with resentment. Lying there, listening to them, I admitted for the first time since Sophie's arrival a year before that this wasn't fun. If they weren't squabbling, they were getting ready to squabble, or so it mostly seemed. In between, they acted out their boredom, expert at making me feel their dissatisfaction. I should have listened to Kris.

All my initial misgivings about dogs in cities came back to me. Even in my two-bedroom apartment, they were like bees in a bottle. They bounced off ceilings and walls, if not physically, then psychically. Keeping the peace, trying to make them happy—that was my existence. I'd become one of the dogs-as-a-way-of-life crowd. I rarely went anywhere, and certainly not to the country; Stanley and I had been tolerated, but not the three of us. No traveling of any kind, despite tempting invitations to events in other countries. Their care, feeding, and entertainment were a full-time job. Egotism, perhaps, but I'd like to think I was put on this earth to do more than that. (Laurie Anderson was asked what she'd take to a desert island, and she didn't name her CD collection or her library. She'd take an agility course to keep her terrier occupied. I understood.)

Wikipedia has an honest appraisal of border terriers, obviously written by someone who knows and loves the breed, noting their ability to remove a squeaker from a toy in seconds flat—no such thing as an indestructible toy around a border—and their predilection for starting a fight if they take a dislike to another dog, no matter the size, or, as Stanley's encounter with the Seeing Eye dog proved, worthiness. Most important, the Wikipedia entry stresses—as Verité Reily Collins does—that borders do best with owners who have long experience of dogs and can devote the time required to satisfy the breed's intelligence and high levels of energy.

The dogs had brought me, if not into the sunlight, certainly into a frame of mind where I could take stock. Stanley and Sophie, separately or together, needed more, much more, than I, a solitary writer, could give them: more people in their lives, longer walks, stretches of time at the beach or in the country to absorb their energy, quell their boredom. I loved my dogs to bits, but I also loved them enough to want better for them.

Other things were nagging at me, not just their discontent. Living on a New York City block, walking a dog, day in, day out, you see people like you. You don't know anything about them other than what you can assume from appearances, but you watch them, dog and owner, grow old together. The dogs age faster, but their owners aren't too far behind. The process occurs as if in one of those nature movies that excited us in the 1950s, a cactus thrusting through the desert floor, blooming, wilting, all in the space of a minute. Humans and dogs stiffen, wrinkle, fade. And then they disappear.

What happened to the woman with the Shar-Pei? She was roly-poly, with plump folds in her face, just like her dog. We'd nodded at each other, our dogs exchanging wary greetings, and I noticed as time went on that she and her dog's folds were sagging in tandem, like waterlogged papier-mâché. And what about the natty fellow and the Jack Russell who both started out upright but became bent, their bodies angling in different directions as if gravity had stepped on them? I already knew what Stanley and Sophie would look like because an ancient border named Hugh sometimes did the rounds with us. He was all bristles and ribs and bony haunches; age had shrunk him, denuded him of muscle. To judge from my relatives, that's the form I'll take. I was comforted to be told that tottery Hugh was still a handful, as are my family in their advanced years.

I found myself questioning all aspects of my life, including whether I wanted to grow old on East Seventy-second Street, to drift into my dotage there, allowing that I wasn't run over by a tram or stepped on by an elephant. A comfortable life, to be sure, and I'd certainly put in hard yards to achieve it. Then again, I was never one to drift. Bump, blunder, crash, maybe, but not drift.

So began a period of anguished tossing and turning, pacing and nail-gnawing, more appropriate for a teenager, not some-one in her mid-fifties; but dignity, like privacy, I decided, is a bourgeois notion. I inched toward a resolution that would have been inconceivable even a month before: to dismantle my life, to change it radically, beginning with Stanley and Sophie. I would find a couple or a family for each of them, people with more resources than I had. Their new parents would have to be as dotty about the dogs as I was, as understanding of their singularity. If I was lucky, I might even have visitation rights. For once I would do the sensible, grown-up thing, even if it near killed me. Even if it broke what was left of my heart.

24.

Heebie-jeebies

The dogs weren't the only ones feeling confined. I was confined to the apartment and the neighborhood by memories of my marriage, by places and possessions that triggered the memories. I was always being ambushed, hurtled back into the past. Time, supposedly the great panacea for sorrow, hadn't helped. I wanted badly to be at peace.

My apartment was stuffed to the gunnels with books, paintings, photographs, papers, LPs, CDs, furnishings, and mementoes from both my life and my husband's. Some people can rummage through their remnants with equanimity, but it gives me the heebie-jeebies. It's the past I fear, not the future, as the saying goes. True, some of the remnants can be amusing. On a scrap of paper scrawled in pencil in handwriting I can't identify, I found this:

> *A feminist lady named Kate*
> *Was a mixture of love and hate*
> *She could care for a guy*

Be the delight of his eye
And happily leave him castrate

No doubt written during a long boozy afternoon in a beer garden near Sydney University in the heyday of feminist activism and Vietnam antiwar protests. All the same, I'd much rather dwell on tomorrow.

Money was also a large part of my decision. (Isn't it always?) I had a two-bedroom apartment that had surged in value. The apartment, on the twelfth floor of a building erected in 1923, was quiet and light-filled, with a view of old carriage houses and the copper dome of the Church of St. Jean Baptiste. I enjoyed having space, but I was also tired of the freelance scramble to earn a living, keeping afloat from assignment to assignment, gobbling up the occasional book advance, no pension, no health benefits, no financial safety net. Riding the edge of the knife. I decided to cash in my chips, invest the money, create an income to relieve the pressure. I would keep only what was essential, buy a small perch, a studio if that's what I could afford, in another neighborhood. No room for much of anything but the basics. No room for one terrier, unthinkable for two.

Acquiring possessions is much easier than dispersing them. It took a year of culling. The books went, not all, but thousands of them. They were a vanity, no longer necessary because, courtesy of the Internet, I could access with ease libraries and bookstores of all kinds across the continents. No need for CDs, either. I downloaded my collection, and that was that. As a computer ad on New York's bus shelters declares, GIGS, NOT CLOSETS. Next, the furniture, lovingly acquired. I was a little taken aback to find how much emotion

I'd attached to inanimate objects, to fabric and wood. After that, papers, photographs, letters—all were dispatched.

I still gasp as if punched in the stomach when I think of what I did. Then again, there was a certain satisfaction in all the whittling, the pruning, the goal of minimalism. F. Scott Fitzgerald wrote in a letter to Thomas Wolfe: "You're a putter-in, and I'm a taker-outer." Putter-ins and taker-outers—as good a way as any to classify writers, and I'm in the latter group. Essence, not ornament. I like meaning that is stitched into seams, hidden by linings, secreted in pockets, tucked up sleeves. Given the chance, friends have joked, I'd edit myself out of existence. This was what it sometimes seemed I was doing as almost everything I'd ever valued or invested with meaning was carried out the door. Obliterating myself.

The first to congratulate me was Alan, my accountant, a frisky fellow whose red hair has gone gray apace with mine. "Many of my clients your age should be doing what you're doing," he said. "Deaccessioning. Downsizing. You don't need as much as you think you need. They understand it intellectually. Emotionally, no. They can't do it." Indeed, person after person, on learning what I was attempting, expressed the desire to be rid of possessions, to live a simpler life. Not that they were about to emulate me. The notion of uncluttering your life has wide appeal, as does taking it even further by turning your back on everything familiar and comforting and wandering the world emotionally unencumbered, in search of an enlightened self. Romantic twaddle. The reality is dead scary, liberating but also desolating. Throughout the whole process, some lines by the British poet Kathleen Raine looped through my brain:

I set out in a dream
To go away—
Away is hard to go, but no one
Asked me to stay,
And there is no destination
For away.

25.

Mine. All Mine

The Wikipedia entry on borders comments on a trait I haven't seen singled out before: a catlike sense of independence. They certainly have catlike paws and legs which they like to drape expressively on furniture or over your arm whenever you pick them up, but they are also similar to cats in that they always maintain a proud distancing, if only a fraction, between them and us: "We know the deal, but don't expect us to fall over ourselves in gratitude." It was this feline quality, along with her city-girl moxie, that had already endeared Sophie to two of my friends, James and Christopher. When I mentioned I might be finding new parents for her, they offered themselves without hesitation.

James, an actor, playwright, and activist, and Christopher, my editor at the publishing house Fourth Estate in London and now a full-time writer, live downtown, on Charles Street in Greenwich Village. Sophie went to them for a few days for a trial period. Even in that short time, she transferred her affection. She came back for a week and was decidedly haughty, ready to sort out not just Stanley but me. When James arrived to take her to her new home, she leaped into his lap, chin thrust up, painfully proprietorial. As she sat there, she slowly relaxed, her face melting like a Jim Carrey mask from a mixture of joy and relief: "I *adore* this man. And he's *mine*. All mine."

Away from Stanley, Sophie was much calmer, and her new parents were able to round out her training: no more soiling, no more gaping holes in possessions—but not, it should be noted, before a few cushions and a prized rug went into the trash. Training a dog, especially one past puppyhood, requires a Pavlovian consistency that I was never able to provide. Sophie's one failing: The rambunctious form of play that she and Stanley developed doesn't endear her to other dogs. In the downtown dog runs—we had none near East Seventy-second Street—she barrels at prospective playmates, overwhelming them. Rebuffed, she retreats behind James's and Christopher's legs, a bundle of hurt, the eager girl who tries too hard, and they wince for her as you might for a human child who can't quite grasp the politics of the playground.

Sophie is the proud owner of an array of winter coats and any amount of rawhide bones. Her first coat had a luxurious fur-trimmed hood, but James confessed she found that outfit disconcerting and wouldn't pee or poop when wearing it. Her favorites are a fetching red plaid number with a corduroy collar and, for rainy weather, a mackintosh with a camouflage pattern. She has become a seasoned traveler: summers in Provincetown, a month in New Mexico, Christmas at Sag Harbor. It was on the Sag Harbor sojourn that James and Christopher forgot to bring along the green flashing ball, and such was her despondency that they had it FedExed from the city. Christopher told me about this in case I doubted their devotion: "*That's* how much we love her." She has those boys wrapped around her little paw.

26.

Nooooooooo

Stanley. My Stanley. His new parents are Sigrid and Desmond, also writers who work from home. As with James and Christopher, there are two of them to take up the slack, to absorb all that terrier energy. The decision to give Stanley to them was much harder. They'd seen a photograph of him that I'd e-mailed to a friend, and they sought me out. I remember my first glimpse of them coming toward Stanley and me at the boat pond, a tall couple, unfussy in demeanor, straightforward in attitude, immediately likable. We auditioned, Stanley for them, they for us, meeting in Central Park through the winter months that straddled 2004 and 2005. I vacillated, in more pain than I wanted to admit, but they were patient with me; this alone recommended them.

Finally, on a particularly bleak day toward the end of winter, the world washed of color, I decided to end the anguish. Several months had passed since Sophie's departure, and the bulletins from downtown told only of happiness. "If you really want Stanley, you can have him," I told Sigrid and Desmond. "Take him. Now." We parted on the road above Bethesda Fountain.

For the first few paces, Stanley went with them, uncertain but ready for adventure. And then he understood. He dug in his heels and howled as he never has before or since, a barbed cry, a hurling cry, that fishhooked into my heart: "Noooooooo." Betrayed.

In a short story by William Trevor, "Folie à Deux," two boys place a gentle, obedient dog on a Li-Lo rubber raft and push him out to sea, an experiment of sorts to see if the old mutt swims back to shore. The dog patiently plays his part, and the Li-Lo drifts out of sight: "Far away already, the yellow of the Li-Lo became a blur on the water, was lost, was there again, and lost again, and the barking began, and became a wail." The dog drowns, his body washing up a few days later, and this act of cruelty marks the boys for life. When I read the story, I imagined that the unfortunate dog's wail was much like Stanley's on that final day of our life together. In case I was being melodramatic, I checked with Sigrid, and she remembers that unbearable sound exactly as I do.

"First loves run deep," said Irene when I told her how Stanley had reacted. Irene had been upset with my decision because she knew how much Stanley meant to me and was worried about how I would cope. And she loved him, didn't want him out of her own life. Serendipitously, her dog-walking round was in the same West Side neighborhood as Sigrid and Desmond's cavernous apartment, so she introduced herself to them, dropping in to see Stanley whenever she could to ease the transition, to be greeted with his usual effusiveness.

We thought it best if I didn't visit until he'd properly settled, until they'd all adjusted. It's no small thing, taking on a dog, beyond a responsibility. Three months passed before I went to their apartment. Far from greeting me with joy as he had Irene, Stanley sat back on his haunches, uncertain, overwhelmed. He looked up at me and then over his shoulder at Sigrid and Desmond, then back at me. Slowly he advanced and poked his head between my calves and snuffled: "There you are." After that, he got on with his life, and so did I.

On that visit, Sigrid told me that Stanley had refused to meet their eyes for the first month, disconcerting for them because they are experienced dog people. I'm glad I didn't know because I would've been across the park in a flash to bring him home. Sigrid e-mails me regularly with reports of his progress and adventures, his singularity more than fully appreciated. When their daughter, Alexandra, comes home, Stanley greets her with such gallantry that it makes her feel, she says, like a movie star. For his birthday, the three of them held a party: "*That*'s how much we love him." Over the top, you might think—I'd never had parties for the dogs—but perfectly reasonable.

His new home is close to a Riverside Park dog run, but Stanley does no better than Sophie in this sort of environment, rushing around and commandeering balls, his boisterousness mistaken for aggression. The dogs-as-a-way-of-life gals, who dictate standards of behavior at the run with Taliban fervor, waste no time in communicating their disapproval to Sigrid: *Bad* mother.

Stanley goes to Maine twice a year with Sigrid and Desmond, where Stanley can revel in deliciousness. (A favorite place, Sigrid relates, is a primeval area carpeted with moss, where he is as awed as a peasant in Chartres Cathedral: "Look at this, Ma! Wondrous!") On Stanley's first trip to Maine,

Desmond took him out for his evening walk. In the quickly gathering northern dark, Desmond tripped and fell unconscious into a bog. Stanley stood on the edge and barked. A distance away, neighbors heard him, and after some time had passed and he hadn't let up, they came to investigate. An ambulance was called, Desmond revived. Stanley, precious boy, princeling, hero. That none of this would have occurred if Stanley had not needed to be walked is but a small point.

27.

Manly

Once upon a time, writers, even the manly ones, did not hesitate to attribute thought and memory to their dogs and describe their deep affection for them. Around the middle of the last century, citing science, we didn't just distance ourselves from animals; we severed the tie. It became tacky for an educated adult—that is, anyone aware of the comparative sizes of cerebral cortexes—to write imaginatively about dogs. Even to empathize with them, as Ackerley did so wonderfully and wickedly, was labeled anthropomorphism, now an irredeemable form of emotion.

We are the poorer for our arrogance in every possible way. Dogs are dogs, humans are humans, different species but all of us animals, more alike than dissimilar, not so far apart on the evolutionary scale as we think, wanting the same basics from life: food, love, tenderness, sex, shelter, fun, purpose, companionship. Some of us, soured by the grossness of our own kind, turn the evolutionary scale on its head, arguing for the superiority of dogs. Peter, the softhearted proprietor of Peter's Emporium for Pets on East Seventy-fifth Street, once he'd deigned to speak not just to Stanley but to me, remarked that he'd be happier if the humans tied themselves up outside his store and let the dogs come in alone. He has a point, echoed long ago by Madame de Sévigné: "The more I see of men, the more I admire dogs."

Actually, it was *especially* the manly writers who made dogs their subject. Rummaging in a pile of books ready for garbage collection, Irene found a copy of *The Fireside Book of Dog Stories,* published by Simon & Schuster in 1943, edited by Jack Goodman, with an introduction by James Thurber. It wasn't in the best of condition, being dog-chewed as well as dog-eared, but she thought I'd be interested. Wonderful book, and a revelation. Thomas Mann is in it, along with Jack London, Booth Tarkington, Robert Louis Stevenson, John Galsworthy, W. H. Hudson, Rudyard Kipling, Don Marquis, and Thurber. Kipling expressed best the feeling that runs through all their words: "A man who cares for dogs is one thing, but a man who loves one dog is quite another."

Pantai Berawa

1.

Iffy

Dogs settled, apartment on the market, I set out for Australia in August 2005. I'd left Sydney to live in New York in 1979, but ties to my native country remained despite the passing decades. Family and friends to visit, publishing business to accomplish, a literary festival, a stint as a university guest writer—a month passed without a moment to dwell on Stanley and Sophie. Then I went to Bali, not because it's an island paradise—iffy propositions, island paradises, in my experience—but because my brother, Dare, has a compound at Pantai Berawa, up the coast from the capital, Denpasar, and he'd spoken with great enthusiasm about the eccentric collection of Indonesian vernacular architecture assembled there and filled with artifacts from all over the archipelago. I'd never been to Indonesia or spent time in the tropics, but Pantai Berawa was as good a place as any to begin my new life, to change its patterns. Maybe I could live part of the year there, part in New York. Ideal for a writer.

Balinese homes typically take the form of compounds, as is the case throughout Asia. Structures are separated by function and arranged around courtyards or connected by walkways, walled off from the outside world. While the rest of Indonesia is Muslim, the Balinese are Hindu, and their compounds always include a shrine, often elaborate, to the various gods credited with creating their island. A collection of compounds, and you have a *desa adat,* or village, governed collectively by an association known as a *banjar.* Unique to Bali, *banjars* have the first and last say on all things: religious and secular, social and cultural.

Dare has given his gallimaufry of buildings the name Puri Angsa, or Goose House, after a gaggle of large white geese who crisscross the yard and gardens, file along paths, yellow feet slapping hard earth, aloof and deliberate as conspiring Vatican priests. Geese have agendas. In the three months I spent at Puri Angsa, I came to envy their purposefulness.

2.

Testicle

The first word I learned in Bahasa Indonesian was *anggrek:* orchid. A bounty of them, some reticently graceful, some cheerfully clownlike, propagated by an Italian expatriate who, shrunk by his years in the tropics, looked like a desiccated faun. On my arrival in Bali, as a courtesy to my brother, the expat took me on a tour of his garden. He had a predilection for judging blooms by their intelligence. Taking a hard look at some unsuspecting orchid trying its best, he'd spit out, "Stupid flower!" which put a stop to my indiscriminate oohing and aahing. He also told me, with unmistakable prurience, that the word "orchid" comes from the Greek *orchis,* or "testicle." I'm not sure I needed to know that.

The second word I learned was *sampah*: rubbish. In Bali, empty lots, backyards, and shoulders of roads are dumps, contrasting with the gorgeously tessellated paddy fields and pinneat courtyards and entryways, whisked clean at the beginning of the day and at the end with brooms made from clumps of palm leaves, the wielder bent slightly at the waist, one hand held behind the back, the other flicking the stiff leaves.

Sydney's beaches are golden, the ocean a healing blue; breakers roll and fizz and foam in happy abundance. While some of Bali's beaches are picture-postcard white, many are inky with ground lava, legacy of long-ago volcanic convulsions. In the rainy season, the tides throw up straggling hillocks of first-world trash on these beaches, like threads of vomit on pavement after a party. The sand sticks like glitter glue. Some believe that Westernization and its debris have caused the gods to desert the island. *The gods are dead chak chak chak.*

3.

Flâneurs

Bali has an indigenous dog that looks like a collie and comes from Kintamani, up near Mount Batur in the center of Bali. The Kintamani breed aside, the majority of Bali dogs are like all third-world canines: not so much dogs as impressionist blobs. Eons of crossbreeding in a limited genetic pool have produced featureless creatures. I averted my eyes whenever I saw these pye-dogs—pariah dogs—lazing on the sides of the *gangs* and *jalans*—lanes and streets—because most were scrofulous, the males with brutish eyes, the bitches with dugs hanging to the ground. These dogs were champions at avoiding the hurtling, swarming moped traffic, a skill they practiced with sublime nonchalance. Bali's flâneurs.

On my second night in Bali, one of these unfortunates crept into my bathroom, bringing with it the thick stink of putrefaction. Trying to discover the source of the smell, I found the creature huddled in a corner, its beseeching eyes fixed on me. Too bloody much! Paranoid that the dog had singled me out—Bali is that kind of place—I called for help. The dog was evicted, the floor disinfected.

4.

Guffaws

The next day I was invited to a ceremony for a sickly infant belonging to a family in a house on the *gang* leading to Puri Angsa. Religion, for better or worse, permeates every part of life in Bali. The ceremony that day, held in a stepped courtyard, was presided over by a blubbery *pedanda*—a Hindu priest, always from the Brahman caste—and featured a solo *topeng* dancer. *Topeng* is a ritual dance drama through which myths as well as political messages are transmitted. The dancer at that ceremony, who changed his gaudy masks and outfits behind a makeshift curtain with goggling children peeking through the cracks, was burlesque in his movements and produced guffaws from his audience.

The priest droned, the *topeng* dancer cavorted, the gamelan band plinked, the Balinese beamed. The brother of the host, a serious young man, stick-skinny and dressed in the immaculate white of the *pemangku,* a lesser level of priesthood open to non-Brahmans, fell into a trance. He shuddered and jerked, collapsed to the ground, opened his eyes. One of the elders gave him an encouraging pat.

Bali was the first stop on the hippie trail when I was at university in Australia in the sixties, and this ceremony was the kind of exotic experience that had attracted the tie-dyed set. They smoked weed and put LSD tabs under their tongues, the better to appreciate—*groove*—on the lushness of the place, the opposite of stodgy Australia, which in those years was so dreary it could have been an outer suburb of London. Bali now attracts vacationing middle-class Australians and moneymen from Asia's banking centers who want a handsome holiday home and obliging servants.

Around the hippies, gory political events were unspooling: In 1965—following a CIA-backed coup in Jakarta and helped along by famine, a volcanic eruption, and a failed attempt by socialists to redistribute land—the Balinese turned on one another and anyone else they resented, such as Chinese merchants, murdering in several weeks a greater proportion of the population than was killed by Pol Pot in Cambodia. Rivers bobbed with heads, history's macabre apples. Underneath the carefully cultivated tourist image of Bali as the Island of the Gods, behind the sweet smiles and gentle manners, is a complex reality fed by a brutal colonial history and an ages-old caste system: the usual human mess.

Offerings—food, flowers, woven palm leaves—were piled higgledy-piggledy in the middle of the courtyard. I sat on a lower step, wishing for a breeze and ineffectually patting at the runnels of perspiration coursing down my face, down my back. The rainy season had begun, and the heat was so heavy that lifting your head to view the horizon was a chore, never mind imagining life beyond it. I was wishing I could forget history, get with the mood of things, enjoy what was proffered. A secular New Yorker to my core, I also hoped that the family was spending money on medical treatment for their thin, pale, colicky baby and not blowing it all on this ceremony.

A rank smell much like the one in the bathroom wafted toward me. I leaned closer to examine the offerings and made out, underneath the clutter, a dead dog, sinews exposed, flesh maggoty. No! The corpse of a sick stray who had met with misadventure? Unfortunately that wasn't the case, or so I was told. The dog in the pile of offerings had been reared for the express purpose of being dispatched, with due ceremony and a list of instructions, to the spirit world, where it would keep watch on the house. A dog with a job.

5.

Spiv

Some of the buildings at Puri Angsa have the simple lines and grace of Shaker architecture; others are paneled with baroque carvings and painted with carnival colors, faded by the years but still gladdening. The center of compound life is a soaring, open-sided two-hundred-year-old Sumatran grain barn with a traditional *alang-alang* roof—a thick palm thatch—and ancient wide-planked teak floors worn to a pleasing silky smoothness. I had a room there, off to the side of the communal area, and for company I had the spirit figures that decorated it. These ancestral totems were collected by the previous owner of the compound, Pak Aulia, a canny Sumatran teak dealer with a decided taste for the unusual. Life-size and aged to indistinct gray shapes, the figures made me start from surprise when I caught sight of them out of the corner of my eye—I mistook them for humans, an effect helped by the bike helmets sometimes parked for convenience on their heads.

I also had for company a one-year-old Southern pigtailed macaque named Chico, who lived in a monkey-sized tree house a stone's throw from the entrance to the main house.

111

The path to the staff quarters skirted his tree, an expansive tropical oak that provided a view of the compound's gates and overlooked a defile alongside a stream used by neighbors going fishing or in search of bamboo for ceremonial decorations. Nothing much happened at Puri Angsa without Chico knowing about it.

Chico was a spiv, a lout, a clown. More than once I found myself blurting, "Don't be such a monkey, Chico!" With his jutting ears and upthrusting jaw, his laddish sneer and wide-boy braggadocio, he could've played a sidekick role in *The Sopranos*. He'd give himself a ruminative scratch as if considering his options, limited by a chain around his waist, and launch himself into motion, sliding up and down the pole to his house, swinging from anything that could be swung from, shaking anything that could be shook, splashing in his *mandi*—a stone trough for bathing—turning any spare object into a plaything, staging kamikaze attacks on passersby. *It's good to be bad, Daddy!*

Chico was partial to fruit and especially rambutans, peeling off their hairy red skins with the concentration of a sushi chef, smacking his lips and making appreciative yum-yum noises as the translucent flesh was exposed. If his belly was full, he tucked surplus food into pouches in his cheeks for digestion later, making him look goiterish. Now and again his chain came undone, and he went through the compound with the speed of a salamander and the destructive powers of a poltergeist. He was *fast*. If you watched Chico on the loose, it wasn't hard to understand why the Balinese believe that monkeys are inhabited by the spirits of the capricious, mischief-making, yet-to-be-settled dead.

Chico was an adolescent boy through and through, but at

the end of the day, he wanted what we all want: to be comforted, reassured. In his case, this took the form of a couple of
bananas—the dainty variety with yellow flesh—and a cuddle.
He'd eat the bananas and then flop on my lap like a rag doll, his
vast store of nervous energy leaving him like air from a tire.
Relaxed at last, he'd set to examining the fabric of my jeans,
grooming it with exacting care, thread by thread, a monkey's
way of being sociable.

6.

Bubble-Brain

Labor is cheap in Bali—in *all* of Indonesia—and it's not unusual for a large compound to have a staff, ten or so people living on the grounds with their children. At Puri Angsa, they tend to the buildings, garden, vegetable tract, fish pond, poultry, and assorted animals; they act as security, liaise with the *banjar*. Produce that's not used by them or my brother's family and friends is sold at the market and the profits divided among them. They cook and otherwise make life easeful for guests.

Some of the staff come from Java, the island adjacent to Bali and the largest in the Indonesian archipelago; some are Balinese—they form a village within a village. Puri Angsa's tight-knit community is headed by Salim, a bantam rooster of a man, a wiry Javanese with a fine eye for antiques and an intuitive design sense. Salim is intensely proud of Puri Angsa and the order and beauty he has achieved there.

Chico was Salim's charge. Noting that Chico was beginning to bite with force, not breaking the skin but leaving bruises, Salim diagnosed loneliness and pronounced the cure: a girlfriend, a *juanita*. *Juanita?* I thought Salim must have seen a

Mexican movie on the tiny television they all gathered around at night in their quarters, families in the first row, bachelors spilling onto the veranda and viewing it through the door. But no, *juanita* is Bahasa Indonesian for "woman."

Chico's biting was not unusual—all monkeys bite. They don't mean harm, not when they are little. It seemed to me that Chico bit in the same way that dogs mouth our hands, to learn about us from the taste of our skin. I was only guessing; I knew as much about monkeys as I knew about tropical fish, which was to say nothing. But in the month I'd been at Puri Angsa, Chico had become conspicuously antsy—whether from hormones or lack of companionship, who knew?

To obtain a *juanita* for Chico, Salim would have to go to the bird market—Pasar Burung—in Denpasar, where all manner of wildlife is sold. He asked if I would like to come along. Of course! I'm one of the few people who like Denpasar, an over-flowing Asian city, all need and invention, a surprise around every corner. And, needless to say, I've never been on an expedition to buy a monkey. A new experience! How exotic! What fun! What a bubble-brain! I had no intention of caring for the monkey beyond feeding her occasionally and being amused by her antics, as I did with Chico; full-time caretaking was Salim's province. In short order, however, I became, despite myself, as obsessed with monkeys as I had been with dogs. In short order, my nose was rubbed in the dismaying trade of wildlife for pets, bush meat, and animal experimentation.

Stalls like those in an amusement park line the alleys of Pasar Burung, but instead of cotton candy and shooting galleries, these stalls are crammed with birds, mostly songbirds, for whom Indonesians have a passion—Salim relaxed by chirruping at his collection—but also parrots, owls, and eagles. (One guidebook helpfully suggests that if you want to see Indonesia's rapidly vanishing bird species, you should visit Pasar Burung.) Bats, big brutes, dusty black in color, are crushed into small cages, hanging like clothes in a closet, destined for the cooking pot. (Bat tastes like duck, or so they say.)

At the stall where Chico was purchased, Balinese monkeys—long-tailed macaques—sat on top of cages, drooping and despondent, their will to live all but extinguished. Some would become pets, while others would be slaughtered for their brains, believed to impart energy. All of them had been poached, their mothers killed. In the middle, a solitary macaque of the same species as Chico, a woebegone baby girl who couldn't bring herself to look at us. Salim bargained, settled on a price of fifty thousand rupiahs (five dollars), and the wee monkey was deposited in a cardboard box secured with string. On the way home, Salim named her Cheeky.

7.

Gila

Cheeky was *bagus sekali*. Exquisite. She was about seven inches high, with huge honey-colored eyes and delicate eyelids, outsize ears that were almost transparent and traced with veins, downy golden-brown fur on her body with a darker Mohawk strip on her head, expressive hands and feet, a tiny abbreviated tail, a little bare bum. The most unsettling feature was her nails, identical to a human baby's.

Spend any time with monkeys, and the obvious thought comes to mind: Darwin had a point. Monkeys are us. They have 94 percent of our genes. They might be notoriously short on impulse control, but so are we. And like us, they use tools and combine sounds for specific purposes and situations. Their intelligence is indisputable. Southern pigtailed macaques— *macaca nemestrina*—can be trained to harvest coconuts and fruit, to know ripeness and distinguish size. Those who live on the edges of civilization are top-notch crop raiders, carrying out their plundering expeditions when farmers are sheltering from rain. They post lookouts, disappearing like wraiths if a warning is sounded.

Despite mounting proof that monkeys talk to one another by combining sounds, researchers are reluctant to admit that they have any kind of syntactical ability. "Because there is no evidence that the calls are words or even wordlike," argued animal-communication expert Marc Hauser in the *New York Times,* "the connection to language is tenuous." This obtuseness reminded me of another researcher, also duly reported in the *Times,* who made the earth-shattering announcement that dogs have emotions, to which dog owners could only say, "No kidding!"

Cheeky was ever so cute, ever so adorable. She was also awash with wretchedness, twitchy with terror. Salim set up a tree house for her in front of his quarters where he could keep an eye on her. A *mandi* was placed on the ground below her house, along with a stone platform for food. As with Chico, a long chain was attached around her middle, the other end to a ring on the pole that led up to her house, where she retreated whenever anyone approached, pushing out her lips in what's called a pout-face, a macaque's way of displaying alarm and aggression.

She made an exception for me. Whenever I came to visit her, she sat with her hands and feet curled around her chain, her eyelids heavy, in an attitude of defeat. I whispered a greeting—"Hello you"—and she ducked her head and gave me a doubtful, sad smile. I rubbed her tummy, and slowly, slowly, she listed over until she lay on her side, eyes closed. Whenever I left, she grabbed hold of my pant leg. I gently loosened her grip, but she followed me to the end of her chain, crying all the while, a thin, high-pitched, steady, piteous lament. A sound I hope never to hear again. A never-ending susurrus of complaint and dispossession.

Cheeky was not only grieving the loss of her mother, who would have fed and groomed her, loved and reassured her, kept her out of harm's way, taught her all she needed to know, but her grandmothers, aunts, sisters, and cousins, the twenty or so females with whom she'd have spent her life. Female pig-tailed macaques stay in their natal troops, with the males migrating to other troops or becoming loners.

I could no more give her back her mother, her troop, her patch of jungle, than pull on Wellingtons and take Stanley and Sophie to a farm in the border country of England. Cheeky's plight tapped directly into the sadness that had accumulated in me. My stiff upper lip, kept as firmly in place as possible since my husband's death, went slack. I started to cry and couldn't stop. I was reduced to quoting W. B. Yeats's romantic lines: *Come away, O human child! / To the waters and the wild / With a faery, hand in hand, / For the world's more full of weeping / than you can understand.*

In between blubbering, I was angry. Cheeky had decided I would be her mother, not a role I wanted, not after my husband's illness, not after the dogs. I'd talk out loud to myself: "Oh, man, how did this happen? I don't want to be anyone's mother, much less a frigging monkey's!" Salim and the others averted their eyes: *Orang gila.* Crazy person. *Bule gila.* Crazy white person.

8.

Ploy

Chico became jealous of Cheeky. If he saw me take the path that led to Cheeky's house, he shot up the trunk of his tree as high as he could go, grabbed hold of a branch with one hand, and leaned out like a sailor on a topmast. From there, he could see over the fences that lined a narrow canal, past a *bale*—a sleeping pavilion—and a garage, to Cheeky's house in front of the staff quarters. Monkeys have enviable eyesight.

Worse, he imitated her piping. The only way to stop their crying was to fasten Cheeky by her chain to a palm tree close to Chico but out of his reach. He was too excitable for them to be together; there was no mother to clip him upside the head when he got out of line. One of the problems with raising monkeys without their mothers is that no one teaches them right from wrong. If Cheeky has a child—female macaques don't come into sexual maturity until around four years of age, and the males at six years; so much for the *juanita* idea—the like-lihood of her abusing her child is high, according to primate researchers. Being a mother doesn't come naturally to monkeys any more than it does to our species; they need examples, and Cheeky wouldn't have any.

With Cheeky out of reach, Chico resorted to various tactics to get close and attract her attention. He lay on his stomach at the end of his chain and stretched as far he could, making vain efforts to grab Cheeky's tail. After a bit he realized that wasn't going to work and embarked on a frantic display of branch-shaking and show-off acrobatics. Through all this, Cheeky remained unimpressed, turning her back to him and calmly prospecting under stones or in the bark of a palm tree for insects, picking delicately with thumb and forefinger, holding up her finds to inspect them before putting them in her mouth. While motherhood might not come easily to her, she certainly seemed to know how to wind a boy up.

Her crying was real, while his seemed more an attention-seeking ploy, but I wouldn't have put playacting beyond her, either. In the next two months, the remaining time I spent in Bali, Cheeky learned to be accepting of everyone except Salim. He was the one who, on that fateful first day, handed over the rupiahs, placed her in the cardboard box, and held her while the vet gave her an injection. Whenever Salim appeared, she backed up, made a pout-face, and chittered in agitation, no matter the kindness he showed her. After a time, though, as her confidence grew, instead of retreating, she scampered after him, pout-facing like a demon. I swear she was also smiling.

9.

Creeping Things

It was a small miracle that Cheeky lived beyond sunset the day we brought her home. I learned that vendors at Pasar Burung fill the monkeys with sugar water and caffeine to give them a semblance of life. I heard of a woman who bought a monkey only to have it die as soon as she got home. This was repeated two more times. The fourth time she returned to the bird market, the vendor said, "I have something else for you," and pulled up some floorboards. Hidden away in the dark crawl space were a baboon and a baby Sumatran tiger, both on endangered lists.

The higher the Indonesian official, the grander the army general, the rarer—and more endangered—the species that's presented to them as tribute; it is not unusual to find orangutans, gibbons, tigers, bears, and civets stashed away in backyards. Now and again an army general placates conservationists by giving up, say, an orangutan, neglecting to say that he had two to begin with. Efforts to close down the bird markets only drive animal poachers underground.

In her first few days with us, we fed Cheeky fruit and vegetables, which she sampled with discernment, a bon vivant in the making, but always wound up spitting out; her stomach wasn't ready for solids. She prospered on a bottle filled with baby formula, sucking to her heart's content. It took us a while to realize she wasn't digesting solids, so perhaps I was being anthropomorphic in attributing her crying to the loss of her mother. She might simply have been hungry.

If Cheeky is lucky, she will live into her twenties. If she's lucky. There are plenty of threats, among them owls who whooshed through the main house and frightened the heck out of the Indonesians, neon-green mambas and shiny black scorpions that frightened the heck out of me. I wasn't fond of the local geckos, either, big rubbery, corpse-colored brutes the size of iguanas and noisy as stock-exchange floor traders. *Creeping things, and flying fowl.*

The habits of creatures led me to teach Salim two new English words, "nocturnal" (owls, scorpions, geckos) and "diurnal" (monkeys). He walked around repeating them for several days because he liked stretching his mouth on their fat vowels. The monkeys disappeared at nightfall into their little tree houses as if they were cuckoo-clock figures, but one evening, in a furious storm, Chico refused to go into his, instead sitting in the whipping rain and screeching and jabbering like the scared monkey he was. A day later, a seven-foot snake, scales patterned in vivid diamonds, was found curled in a big earthenware pot—a pot on whose rim Cheeky liked to balance in those sessions when she teased Chico with her aloofness.

Salim let slip that *garam*—salt—would deter snakes, much as it deters slugs and snails and causes dogs' limbs to seize up in the winter in New York. He humored me and spread copious amounts of it on the ground under the monkeys' tree houses. No doubt it dissolved in the first rainfall.

10.

Miss Kate

Doesn't Understand

Cheeky found a soul mate, Putu, a village crazy woman, who sat companionably with the macaque, feeding her string beans, both of them at peace for the moment. Putu was a mute who wandered the village and appeared now and again to commune with the spirit figures in the main house. Reed-straight, wearing a batik sarong and a jacket, a scarf tying back her graying hair, she'd circle the floor, gliding over the ancient teak, reaching to stroke the ancient wood, respect and wonder in her every move.

Putu's appearances nearly always startled me because she seemed to materialize out of nowhere. Her routine never varied. A smile by way of greeting, and then she drifted off to the spirit figures. One day, though, to my enormous surprise, she ignored the figures and gathered up a mango from a pile of fruit, a cigarette from a pack on the table, and a copy of the *New Yorker,* and settled in for a nosh, a smoke, and a good long read. To judge from her smile, the cartoons appealed.

Barsori, a personable young Javanese with a broad face and stocky body, came into the house. I pointed at Putu and asked, "She understands English?" He told me that she'd been a famous Legong dancer in her time and could speak excellent English before she became a mute. "What happened to her?" I asked. "Why is she crazy?" Barsori answered by making hard, swooping motions with his hand, repeatedly slashing the air. "Her husband. He hit her," he said, in case I'd missed his meaning.

Barsori, who was from Salim's home village in Java, played chess with me every evening. He was good at the game, and I was terrible. He'd make a move and then look at me pityingly and ask, "Miss Kate maybe doesn't understand?" I'd answer, "You're right, Barsori. Miss Kate doesn't understand. Please explain." Barsori, who was parentless in a culture where family is everything, was aching to marry his sweetheart, but he had no money, having fecklessly invested in the coolest kind of moped—a laddish two-stroke gas-guzzler. His girl lived in his old village, too far away to visit except once a year, during the month of Ramadan. She wasn't beautiful, Barsori confessed, but she had a good heart, which was what mattered most to him. Loneliness was the theme of our conversations, small Javanese, big Anglo, as we squinted at the chess board in the weak light, geckos straddling the beams above our heads, calling to each other in full throat: *ek-ak ek-ak ek-ak.*

The old Sumatran grain barn, sheltered from the elements by the overhang of its *alang-alang* roof, was open on three sides. Because theft is a problem in Bali, I barred my door at night. As a further precaution against intruders, Barsori slept outside, disturbingly like a vassal but comically hard to wake.

Invariably, on Saturday nights, we would hear commotion and see flashing lights at the luxury villas on the other side of the river at the bottom of Puri Angsa's garden: *shabu-shabu* boys—ninja-robed Javanese youth high on heroin-laced methamphetamine—making raids. Luxury villas in paradise have high walls topped with glass.

The spirit figures are said to protect Puri Angsa from intruders. As well, the compound is folded into the village, and members of the *banjar* come at a run, armed with sticks and machetes, if a drum is beaten. Most houses have one of these drums, a hollow length of wood suspended from a tree or rafter, that makes a distinctive woodpecker sound when banged with a length of bamboo: *pok-pok-pok-pok*. All the same, I'm not sure which is the stronger power—spirit figure, *banjar,* or heroin-laced methamphetamine.

11.

Pissing into the Wind

Puri Angsa's little community normally heaped attention on Chico and Cheeky, but during Ramadan, many of them were preoccupied with prayers, fasting, making amends, visiting family. Taking turns, they trekked home to Java, loading up their mopeds with bundles and baskets, a child wedged here and there, transforming the flimsy bikes into motorized turtles. The monkeys grew ever more plaintive and resentful. I tried to pay them no attention, without success. I'd blundered into their world through ignorance and thoughtlessness, and I wanted to put it right. Instead of spending their lives with chains around their waists, perhaps Cheeky and Chico could be placed in a primate sanctuary. I'd heard of a nearby group concerned with the survival of the Sumatran orangutan. Someone there might have a suggestion.

Salim drove on my outings, and Warsi, who was in charge of cooking at Puri Angsa and spoke the best English, came along as translator. Warsi, tiny and tenderhearted, also guided me across streets, my freckled hand firmly in her brown one, because the insane traffic invariably left me flapping on the curb, a scarecrow without a crop. The director of the orangutan organization, a young American, told me she'd once hired a taxi to go from one side of a particularly daunting Jakarta thoroughfare to the other, which made me feel sisterly until she showed no interest in Chico and Cheeky. She all but yawned in my face. Unlike orangutans, pigtailed macaques are not endangered, merely "vulnerable"; the Sumatran ape population has been halved in ten years, while macaques have been diminished by 20 percent. Better that Cheeky had been eaten than spend her life chained or in a cage, the director suggested, which wasn't what I wanted to hear.

Undeterred by my frostiness, she embarked on the donor pitch for her organization: Orangutans are the ambassadors of the Sumatran jungle—jungle that is the "lungs" of the region but has been decimated by two thirds in the past twenty years for its timber and to establish vast palm-oil plantations. Ubiquitous in foodstuffs and health products, palm-oil usage will likely soar because it isn't a hydrogenated fat. Even more ominously for the orangutan, palm oil shows promise as a biofuel. A double-edged sword. Both Sumatran orangutans and their sister species in nearby Borneo, the director informed me, will be extinct by 2010. To underline further the dire plight of these lordly apes, she flicked on her computer and scrolled through endless stomach-turning pictures of mangled or impaled orangutans and their babies in the middle of rolling groves of stubby oil palms.

All true. A tragedy. Orangutanacide. Actually, considering the question of genes, genocide. Apes share even more genes with us than monkeys: 98 percent. I asked the director if her organization was approaching corporations for funding. She looked at me as if I'd grown two heads. Consorting with the enemy? One good lecture deserves another, so I pushed on: Australian insurance companies, for example, are only too aware of what will happen if the "lungs" of Southeast Asia disappear. Don't speak truth to power—power couldn't care less. Instead, speak money. Show the downside to shareholder value from shortsighted business practices.

By then I'd grown three heads, not two. The director saw a dippy tourist who'd bought a monkey and had a lightbulb go on in her head. I saw a humorless do-gooder living up to a stereotype, one who wouldn't know Milton Friedman from Amartya Sen. When it comes down to it, though, we weren't that different: She was chained to her convictions, and I was caged by my contradictions.

Indonesia has homegrown conservationists who are trying to promote sustainable forestry and to establish industries that don't harm the environment, but they are contending with overpopulation, corruption, lack of education, religious fundamentalism, and perpetually shifting tectonic plates that cause earthquakes and tsunamis—problems that are as intertwined and intractable as a bale of barbwire. Also, the Chinese economic juggernaut is moving into the region on a scale that will make the rubber and sugarcane plantations of colonial times look puny. You could say that conservationists are pissing into the wind.

On the way home, we came across some rat bikers lazing against a fence and having a gossip, their ingenious *Mad Max* vehicles covered with handfuls of grass to keep them cool in the sun. Rat bikes are cobbled together from discarded parts—the front part might be from a Vespa, the back from a Yamaha, and your guess is as good as mine in the middle—the whole left rusty or painted matte black and plastered with stickers. I took photographs of the bikers and praised their bikes—*begus sekali!*—trying hard not to notice that the bikes were embellished with monkey skulls.

12.

What if Soldiers,
Swallows, Stopped

My brother advised me to forget about monkeys and go shopping—Bali is a vast Pier 1 store, stuff galore. One of his friends suggested another kind of diversion: a Brazilian lover. Balinese men are too enmeshed in their families for the role of gigolo, but Brazilians, part of Bali's large expatriate population, are happy to service the women tourists. They have a good line in sweet-talking, I'm told. Dignity might be bourgeois, but self-respect isn't. Instead, with Salim in tow, I went to the Bali Zoo.

The Bali Zoo is an unfortunate time capsule. It's the way Sydney's Taronga Zoo and other Western zoos used to be: small cast-iron and concrete enclosures containing an arbitrary selection of sickly or bored creatures. The idea was to show Salim the primate cages so he could build one for Chico and Cheeky. If they had to be in captivity, a cage would allow them to be unchained part of the day. We found the macaques, a number of species, all housed individually in cages that at least made up in height what they lacked in width. An adult female *macaca nemestrina* pecked away at a crumbling log that had pockets of insect life, a diversion that Salim duly noted, along with the various apparatuses for swinging and climbing.

The female macaque gave me pause: This is what Cheeky would look like when grown up, not cute and adorable but large and chunky, with a bosom and a lumpy, estrus-swollen red bottom. When the macaque wasn't excavating insects, she was shoving her bottom in the face of the male macaque in the adjoining cage, which was driving him spare because there wasn't anything he could do about it. Baby and adult macaques, it turns out, could not be more different. Without training, the adults can be as destructive as baboons, which are currently making life difficult for humans in South Africa, according to a Durban newspaper: "Unruly gangs are raiding the expensive homes that line the spectacular coast of South Africa's Cape Peninsula, clearing out pantries, emptying fridges, and defecating over the designer furnishings." Oh dearie me.

Another section housed gibbons, those graceful long-armed creatures that, like orangutans, are near extinction. Gibbons are classified as apes, not monkeys, although their smallish size causes them to be confused with the latter. They live in treetops and are known not only for their acrobatics but for their call, a high-pitched hooting that sometimes takes the form of a contrapuntal duet. These lyrical sounds, the sonic equivalent of the gibbons' vaulting motions, carry for miles, making it easy for poachers to find them: Their body parts are in demand for traditional medicine. Salim and I watched in appreciation as the gibbons looped around their cages. While we stood there, heads upturned, a lone gibbon, separated from four gibbons of another species by a concrete wall, climbed to the topmost corner next to the wall and reached a hand through the cage bars. A gibbon on the other side responded by doing likewise to grasp the extended hand. And there they sat, without moving, hands entwined. *What if soldiers, swallows, stopped. What if oceans. But they don't.*

13.

Puckered

In an attempt to stop my blubbering, Salim and Warsi took me to Pura Tanah Lot, a temple on an outcropping in the sea. They led me through the jumble of tourist concession stalls that line the path to the temple, urging me to the edge of a crumbling cliff, the better to see the ancient structure, which seemed, on that desultory rainy-season day, to be so worn by weather to insignificance that it could slip beneath the waves at any moment with only a small gasp.

From that vantage point, the coastline stretched for miles in either direction. The sea was dull black, bolts of faded fabric razored by long, sharp breaks, puckered by unforgiving currents, bulging with swells and surges. The Balinese fear the sea, as well they might, and few learn to swim; they are forever appeasing it and the demons who live in it.

At my feet, a mangy mutt had curled up for a snooze in a depression in the pitted rock. Farther below, a man was digging for sea serpents in the wet sand.

14.

Numb

In the mornings, I'd ask Salim, "Is it going to rain today? *Hujan?*" And he'd answer "Maybe" or "Positively." On October 1, 2005, a Saturday, he'd said, "Maybe." Early that evening, as I stood under the overhang of the *alang-alang* roof watching the light fade and wondering when the *shabu-shabu* boys would start their raids, I heard faint thunder in the distance. I bent my neck to scan the sky and see what kind of storm was in the offing. No clouds. Suicide bombers from Jemaah Islamiyah, an al Qaeda–financed Malaysian terrorist group, had targeted the seafood restaurants at Jimbaran Bay, where people eat at tables on the sand and watch the sun set over the Indian Sea. Twenty were killed and ninety wounded. Although the quarry was "all white people," the immediate casualties of this jihad were mostly Indonesians. *As-salamu alaykum.* Peace be upon you.

The bombers chose Bali because it would have "global impact," according to plans retrieved, along with a list of potential targets, after Azahari Husin, the group's Malaysian bombmaker, was killed in a raid. To be sure, although "the body count" wasn't as high as the nightclub bombings in 2002, when

202 people perished, the international media reported the tragedy, and it was filed, along with other such bombings, in the consciousnesses of people all over the world under the heading of "Welcome to Life in the Twenty-first Century." The real impact, though, was local. One bombing is grievous; two is a series, more to come. The Balinese economy is dependent on tourism; the island was enveloped in despair as the hotels emptied and sales of villas stalled. Everywhere, numb faces, gorgeous smiles extinguished.

At the Bintang supermarket and the Bali Deli, both on Azahari Husin's hit list because they are patronized by *bules,* police started going over cars with bomb detectors. Unsettling, to say the least. The consensus was that this was for show and the police would soon disappear, as they had after the last bombing, but no, they stayed, and the tourists stayed away. Azahari Husin's ringleader cohort, another Malaysian, Noordin Mohammed Top, remains at large. And despite reassurances of religious moderation, an increasing number of Indonesian Muslims are choosing the name Osama for their boys.

15.

Maybe

I decided to leave Pantai Berawa, return to New York. Iffy propositions, island paradises.

"Will you come back, Miss Kate?" Salim asked.

"Maybe," I replied, thinking, Not bloody likely!

"Positively!" he said, his face shining with the pride he felt for Puri Angsa.

"Maybe," I repeated, trying hard to return his goodwill.

Picking up on my reluctance, Salim added, "*Pelan-pelan, Miss Kate.*" Go slow. Take it easy. Advice he often had occasion to give me.

"I hear you, Salim," I replied, although what I wanted to say was "I am as I am." Prévert—*Je suis comme je suis / Je suis faite comme ça*—or Popeye—*I yam what I yam*—same sentiment. Secular New Yorker. Big sook. Feminist lady named Kate.

16.

A Secondhand Emotion

For someone who prides herself on not being a softie, I spent a lot of time crying in 2005. Indeed, on the way home from the Bali Zoo, Salim was emboldened to ask if everyone in New York had wet faces. (He could have been referring to my copious *bule* perspiration and not tears.) I had left New York thinking I'd discovered a truth: The heart is finite. Mine wasn't parched and dried up—it was in bits, broken beyond repair; shards. Nonsense, of course. The heart—mine, at any rate—seems infinitely able to restore itself, to break again. What comes to mind is the cut-and-come-again pudding of an Australian children's book that was staple reading for my generation. The pudding, which belongs to a pair of swagmen—tramps—can regenerate after every helping, making it priceless and the target of dastardly pudding thieves.

Heart in bits? Broken beyond repair? Pudding thieves? In my defense, let me quote Tina Turner: *What's love but a second-hand emotion?* "Show, don't tell" is a cardinal rule of fiction writing, and like all rules, it's meant to be broken. That noted, the irrational, bottomless nature of yearning, banal and mawkish almost by definition, is better shown than told, better addressed obliquely than head-on, unless you have the wit and intelligence of John Donne or can set it to a melody. Unless you are Joe Cocker. Still, I loved my dogs, and my heart went out to the monkeys. When we cry for our animals, we cry for the whole sodding mess. The whole sodding, sorry mess.

New York

1.

And I Thank the Lord
I'm Not, Sir

Murderous. That was my mood back in New York. I tripped on a low step, turning my foot into a fat purple sausage, and spent most of the summer of 2006 with my leg propped on pillows, or maneuvering clumsily on crutches around an apartment stripped of most of its furnishings, everything else in cardboard boxes. I had no choice but to go slow, take ample time to contemplate life's tedious lessons. *Pelan-pelan*—phooey.

I was still in my apartment, unable to move because the board of my building had rejected a buyer for the apartment. Anyone who lives in a New York apartment building knows about these governing entities, elected by owners to allocate spending and decide on the eligibility of buyers. The intensity of the disputes over decisions can produce lifelong enmities. I'd wake in the middle of the night, my foot hurting like hell, fulminating about the board—fiduciary responsibility? ha!—until I was in danger of imploding from anger. Along with politics, real estate was dominating thought and conversation in New

York, an obsession captured by an artist, Jessica Diamond, with the witty slogan "Buy a Condo or Die." Me, I wanted to sell a condo and live.

The other bane of New York apartment life is burst plumbing, especially in old buildings like mine, where the original pipes were galvanized iron, now clogged or rotted or both. The ceiling in my bathroom started blistering, as did the adjoining wall in the bedroom. They had to be opened up, the cause of the leak discovered, industrial dehumidifiers installed to hasten the drying, a process that took months. The apartment reeked of mold. Outside, the hallways were being renovated, and white plaster dust seeped through and coated what was left of my belongings.

"Isn't it lucky you don't have the dogs," friends and neighbors would say on hearing of my accident, to which I could only grind my teeth. I would have managed, I wanted to say, but they meant well. If I were a God-fearing woman—and I thank the Lord I'm not, sir—I'd think I was being punished.

2.

Whoopee

I also had plenty of time to contemplate the world, going to hell in a handbasket with more cussedness than usual. Talking heads were preoccupied with parsing the Iraq war. Was it another Vietnam? Civil war? Quagmire? All of which begged the question: How was it that Uncle Sam was once again in a terrible jam? Cue the kazoos: *Come on generals, let's move fast / Your big chance has come at last . . . You know that peace can only be won / When we've blown 'em all to kingdom come. . . .* I can't say that I thought highly of Country Joe and the Fish back in the 1960s, but in the summer of 2006 their blackly humorous, foot-stomping music had the perverse effect of cheering me up no end. And then Hezbollah kidnapped two Israeli soldiers, and Israel responded by invading Lebanon. For a few weeks, our age of anxiety was on the verge of turning into an age of all-out hyperventilating panic. This could be it, the beginning of the end: *Whoopee, we're all going to die.*

3.

Whatever the Truth

For my point of view—swollen foot propped on a pillow, ceilings and walls moldy and flaking, building board refusing to budge on their decision, the Middle East conflagrating—the long summer of 2006 was not just an uncomfortable and troubling time but decidedly surreal because macaques followed me back to the U.S. in the strangest form. They made the headlines for weeks when Senator George Allen, a Republican presidential hopeful known for his cowboy comportment, referred to a Democratic Party staffer, a Hindu American, as a macaca at an election rally. After this piece of tin-eared bigotry and general boofheadedness, Allen went from front-runner to ex-senator. The American appetite for faux John Waynes had its limits.

Allen's gaffe took place in what now seems an infinity of news cycles ago, but it stayed with me because it mirrors an incident at the beginning of the Buru Quartet, a spellbinding series of novels by Pramoedya Ananta Toer that traces the rise of the Indonesian movement for independence from the Dutch. The hero of these books is a Javanese who goes by the nickname of Minke, acquired when a Dutch schoolteacher starts to call him a monkey and, more quick-witted than Allen, thinks better of it and changes midword to "minke." No one knows what a minke is, least of all Minke, but the name sticks. Never was a racial slur worn more proudly and to more subversive effect.

Pram, as he was known in Indonesia, spent a large part of his life imprisoned, first by the Dutch and then by the Indonesian generals, who sent him to the scabrous penal island of Buru. The Buru Quartet has a cliff-hanging, *Arabian Nights* quality because Minke's story was originally related aloud by Pram, who wasn't allowed writing instruments, in installments to entertain his fellow prisoners. Gather around, listen up. Pram, who chain-smoked clove cigarettes and had a generous Indonesian grin—his entire face became curly with mirth—was sui generis, an independent thinker and champion of human rights to some, contrarian and pain in the neck to others. Whatever the truth, he insisted on paddling his own canoe, too much so even for the Nobel Prize committee, who failed to give him their prize for literature. Pramoedya Ananta Toer died at the beginning of the long summer of 2006; Minke lives.

4.

Mouthy Bitch

As soon I could hobble without crutches, James and Christopher sent Sophie my way to work her magic. The very sight of her made me smile, relax, think better of the world. That I could walk only at a snail's pace suited her fine: She could sniff and mark everything—women are the new men—to her heart's content. Nothing got her going so much as the blocks of wood placed underneath the metal posts that hold up the scaffolding erected when building facades are being repaired. Seasoned with dog pee, these blocks are reused the length and breadth of Manhattan. To dogs, they are a Smithsonian of smells, a Google news page hyperlinked to neighborhoods from Washington Heights to Wall Street. Choice, *very* choice, deserving of utmost concentration and exaggerated sniffing sessions.

As an experiment, Sigrid brought Stanley over for a reunion. Over a year had passed since the dogs had last seen each other, and the two of them had a jolly time, sloppy kisses, boisterous romping, skidding and wheeling, in complete accord, the best of siblings. The visit was such a success that we got them together again. The second time around, they snarled and squabbled without cease. Nothing could induce them to make peace. It was all too familiar: Stanley wearing his look of pained forbearance, Sophie screwing up her face in disgust, redoubling her determination not to be left out of anything.

I have to admit that Sophie was the major instigator of discord. Win some, lose some, not her motto, at least in regard to Stanley. A week or so later, I came across a fellow with a border identical to Sophie, same short legs, same crooked tail. Her name was Teazer, and her owner and I chatted. I told him about Sophie, her alpha female characteristics. He laughed. "*All* girl borders are alpha females. *All* of them pee with their hind legs in the air," he said. We both glanced down at Teazer, at that very moment straining at her leash, bristling with aggression, close to bursting in her eagerness to get at a cat in a nearby store. "Teazer is mellow compared with my first border," he said. "Now, she was a *real* spitfire."

I remembered encountering in the border terrier literature a breeder who advised prospective owners to consider male puppies instead of female if they wanted a more pliable creature, contrary to received opinion about the gender of dogs. It seems girl borders are infamous for their independent streak. A mental image of the border terrier universe formed: sturdy boys patrolling perimeters, making sure everything is in its place, *bourgeois gentilhommes* to the tip of their carrot-shaped tails, and hot on their heels, never giving them a moment's peace, those pesky girls, those rackety females. If Stanley could talk, he'd say something along the lines of a sentiment expressed by a character in a Bill James mystery and which I hear in one form or the other all the time: "I'm against all sexism, but who let that mouthy bitch in here?"

5.

Clever Britches

Desmond sent me an e-mail, telling me among other things, that he'd discovered that thirty-inch steps, 120 steps to the minute—the U.S. Army marching cadence—was just the right speed for Stanley. Desmond, now a financial writer, spent a few years in the army. And then he added, "Stanley is well, but you aren't. Please try to be. We love him, but he is not lost to you, only away from you."

He was referring to my heart, still hurting over the dogs, not my foot, but he was right: Stanley was not lost to me, and neither was Sophie. I had wanted them to have richer, larger lives, but I'd never expected it to work out for all three of us; I thought I'd always feel bereft. A childhood on an Australian farm produces not only world-class pragmatists but also world-class pessimists. The harsh climate shapes our souls, makes us expect retribution. We learn on our father's knee that the list of things that can cause misery is long. With foes and adversaries such as drought, hail, locusts, dust storms, foot rot in sheep, rust in wheat, city politicians, and heartless bankers, the only thing to do is have a few laughs along the way. Oh, to be happy and redeemed! Fat chance. Squint and you can always see locusts swarming on the horizon.

And yet that's how it turned out, happy and redeemed. The summer ended, my foot healed, I found another buyer, someone who appreciated the apartment for the reasons I had and didn't want to do an instant gut renovation, and this time, with only some tearing out of hair, the deal was done. As for politics, insistently, naggingly on our minds because of the Iraq war, the Republicans lost the midterm elections, although George W. Bush remained as oblivious as ever to opinion and advice—to the point where one commentator said he appeared to be "talking to mirrors and taking instruction from his dog." For their part, the Democrats went into a swivet, reduced to sparrow-farting around, for fear of losing votes if they seemed soft on terrorism.

I moved to the West Side of Manhattan to a fifty-story building that's part of the Lincoln Center complex. New York neighborhoods have such distinct personalities that I feel I've moved to another country, not just across Central Park. My new neighborhood used to be a miscellaneous pocket of buildings—the Lincoln Center concert halls, Fordham University School of Law, television studios—a buffer between the Upper West Side and Hell's Kitchen—but ever since the vast Time Warner Center went up, followed by a frenzied spate of luxury condo construction, it's become a proper neighborhood, international in feel, with newly moneyed Chinese, Indians, and Russians buying along the river, hedge-fund-rich Americans along Central Park. My own building—dogs welcome, no ancient plumbing to spring leaks—is popular with Japanese, opera divas, and jazz luminaries. My apartment is tiny but high up, with a wall of windows that gives me views of the Hudson River and the George Washington Bridge in one direction, Central Park in the other. Best of all, for an Australian who could swim before she could walk, on the fifteenth floor, is a pool of a length to do decent laps.

When James and Christopher are busy, Sophie comes to me. She bosses me around and cuddles up close and knows that if she holds out for roast chicken, roast chicken she will get. James has come to think of me as Sophie's grandmother—her spoil-her-rotten grandmother. Sophie comes bouncing off the elevator and down the corridor with James bouncing along not too far behind. She zooms right by me to check out the apartment, making sure, maybe, that Stanley isn't there and her stash of balls is. James brings with him optimism and formidable energy. He's made it a project to banish the locusts from my horizon. I listen, not always with grace, to his advice about positive thinking. I like my locusts; I've lived with them a long time.

My walks now with Sophie take us around Lincoln Center, always someone or something to gawk at: Pedro Almodóvar and Penelope Cruz at the Walter Reade Theater; clowns from the Big Apple Circus; New York's smartest in evening clothes for the opening of Anthony Minghella's *Madama Butterfly;* serried ranks of giant mannequins draped in flapping rags in a loading bay. These last were props for a production of *The Coast of Utopia,* and they caused Sophie to sit flat on her bottom in amazement. Later, she confided that she is of two minds about Tommy Stoppard's work: "Too much the clever britches, and he does go on." Believe me, she's quite the critic.

Sophie and I see students from Juilliard toting tubas and

other musical instruments in hard-shelled cases, and I derive comfort from the fact that not everyone is playing video games. We also see the African-American and Hispanic kids from Martin Luther King Jr. High School, situated at the back of Lincoln Center. This school gained notoriety as the first in New York to install metal detectors. These days, while the students might not be concealing weapons in their baggy clothes, they're still tough: They tote attitude.

I usually avoid walking Sophie when school lets out because the sidewalks are thronged with kids acting out their freedom as they head toward the subway. One day I forgot, and we found ourselves surrounded by kids punching each other on the arm, trying out insults, flirting with comic abandon. Sophie chose that moment to make little circles on the edge of the curb until she found the right position to poop. She strained and strained until she was finished, and I stood there in that studied way of New York dog owners whose dogs are pooping, plastic bag in hand, looking into the middle distance. A group of girls came by, catcalling and shrieking at a volume calculated to raise the hackles of luxury condo owners. A tiny gal, temerity from top to toe, broke away from her friends when she drew opposite Sophie and me. She looked at Sophie, looked at me, and said, "Eat that shit."

6.

"That's Our Dog"

David Mamet has a larger point to make when he observes that terriers find their joy in going down burrows after rodents. Humans are similarly hardwired, he writes, for narratives. Stories—they're what give us joy, the ones we tell ourselves or the ones that are told to us. They soothe us, give shape to emotions, make sense out of happenstance and chaos, loose ends and loss. Laugh, cry, stave off boredom. I hadn't known this, but James's story about Sophie coming into his life was one of instant enchantment, as it was for me:

> *Did I ever tell you what was going through my mind the first time I met you and Sophie and Stanley? The moment I walked into your apartment, I knew that Sophie was mine. I've heard people talk about this pet-owner phenomenon. They walk into a pound or shelter or store, and they just seem to know which dog is theirs. I'd always been dubious about such Love-at-First-Sight stories, chalking them up to wishful thinking or romanticizing the past so that they could justify their love. But with Sophie, I knew right away that she was mine.*

You left the room at one point, and Sophie was sitting in my lap. I turned to Christopher and said, "This is our dog." Normally, I don't go around coveting other people's dogs, especially someone I've just met. Christopher said, "Well, maybe a dog like Sophie." "No," I told him, "this dog. She's ours." Christopher and I had been pretending that we owned a dog; we were practicing what it felt like to care for an animal without having to deal with the inconveniences of walking and feeding the thing. We called our pretend dog George Eliot, and in this way we bypassed the need to assign gender and at the same time we kept our favorite writer in mind.

But made-up dogs have their limitations, and by the time I met Sophie I was primed for the real thing. It may be ridiculous to posit such a notion, but I feel that Sophie was ready for me as well. Whatever understanding passed between Sophie and me that first evening, it found its footing some months later when you asked if we'd be interested in giving her a home. After that we were off and running—literally. I can't thank you enough for making my fantasy a reality. And isn't this what dogs do for us? They take us out of our brains and down into the street, where we are more real, more vivid; their attention keeps us in place and allows us constant contact with the sensate world in which we live.

7.

Inconsequential

Stanley is neither lost to me nor far away. In fact, he lives within walking distance of my new apartment. We've taken to meeting—Sigrid, Stanley, and I—at the new pier that unfurls on the Hudson River near Riverside Park. In the winter, it's brisk down there, with a wind of a strength that could quite possibly scoop us up and deposit us in New Jersey. Dirty ice slops against derelict ironwork structures and rotting wooden pilings, remnants of the industries that once lined the Hudson. In the summer, though, the pier becomes festive, donning the equivalent of a Hawaiian shirt, with a café serving hamburgers and beer at tables with umbrellas, bowls filled with ice water for dogs. Some people buy their food, others bring picnics. If it weren't for the giant pylons bearing the West Side Highway above us and the steady hum of coursing traffic, we could imagine ourselves at a seaside resort.

Still, this is what we have available to us, and we think it's mighty fine. Irene sometimes comes up from the East Village to join the three of us, and we hang out there, sometimes for hours, Stanley periodically changing laps, royalty deigning to give commoners equal time. We chatter, gossip, joke. Dogs, politics, and real estate feature in our conversation. Work occasionally comes up—Irene's plans now that she has completed a social work degree; the progress of a book Sigrid cowrote on espionage during World War II—but mostly we embrace the inconsequential. Or we try to. The thing is, we are of an age when hanging out is foreign to us. We've long ago forgotten how to be idle, shoot the breeze, chew the fat. We've turned into Lewis Carroll's White Rabbit: *Oh my ears and whiskers, how late it's getting!* For the first half hour I have to force myself to stay still, and Sigrid reports the same. Bit by bit, though, doing nothing is growing on us. For stretches at a time, the static in our brains—that rhubarb of noisy emotion—is muted.

Blame it on Stanley. He gives us a reason to meet, to be friends, and, it would seem, to be lazy. Stanley's idea of heaven is to have Sigrid, Irene, and me in the same room. Or under the same umbrella. When this happens, his habitual vigilance melts away. He basks in our adoration. Stanley's harem.

8.

National Calamity

The sensate world in the form of a green door is impinging on Sophie. She knows this door and what's behind it, and she's freaking: "No way!" Sophie is usually fearless. The only time I've seen her back down from anything was when an Afghan hound lunged at her. Sophie stood her ground until he lunged again, at which she calmly turned tail and walked away at a steady if rapid clip down the block, as if she'd just remembered she had business elsewhere. The minute we rounded the corner, she slowed to her normal pace. Out of Dodge.

The door belongs to the row house where Richard, the dog stripper trained by Kris, lives. I'm taking Sophie, shaggy as a sheep and now squirming like the devil, to her biannual grooming session because James is busy with a project in New Orleans and Christopher is finishing a draft of a book. Sophie doesn't mind being brushed or bathed, and Richard is the gentlest of fellows, which makes her aversion to coming here mystifying. James thinks it's because Richard has his stripping table in the basement, an excellent place for it because the dog hair quickly thickens the air, but it's gloomy, with dark corners and piles of the sort of unidentifiable objects that end up in basements. And Richard has a distinctive German accent. You'd think, the way Sophie's heart is beating, that we're about to enter Transylvania.

Richard, a hale septuagenarian, opens the door. He's beaming because he's cradling in his arms a Norwich terrier, a four-month-old named Chloe. His look is familiar: He's besotted. We make our way down creaky stairs, and Chloe curls up while Sophie, with reproachful looks at me, submits to Richard's ministrations. She calms down, lulled by our conversation. I haven't seen Richard since the dogs left me nearly two years ago; we have catching up to do.

"Why did you decide on a Norwich?" I ask. When I last saw him, he was considering a border to replace a dog who had died.

"A border at my age? No." He shakes his head. "They need too much exercise." He knows dogs.

I'm all attention when Richard tells me he has been to Crufts, the largest and best-known dog show in the world, held in Birmingham, England. "I had to go once in my life," he says. "Six thousand dogs. Can you imagine?" I can't. Apparently the judging gets complicated, if not downright internecine. He watched the border competition and was surprised by how different English borders were compared with those bred in the United States. The English borders are more uniform in size, keeping close to the standard with regard to weight, which should top out at around fifteen pounds for males and fourteen pounds for females, with medium bones and narrow chests to match. Border breeders in the United States aren't always quite as respectful of the standard.

The debate about the size of borders has been going on

ever since the breed was registered. Verité Reily Collins quotes a choleric letter to a dog magazine from the 1920s: "It is a thousand pities to see Borders of 17 and 18 lbs on the show bench, but it is nothing short of a national calamity when it comes to the matter of work. What use is a big Terrier with wide shoulders to go down our narrow drains [after rats]?" *National* calamity, no less, and some would still agree. Sometimes a border will get wedged down a hole or warren and have to be dug out, but as one of the great border breeders, Jack Price of Oxcroft, dryly observed of the new big-boned show terriers: "You want a spade to put them in, not to dig them out."

Richard tells me he thinks that Norwiches bred in the United States are, all things considered, better than those he saw at Crufts, an opinion he delivers looking fondly back over his shoulder at Chloe, who is sound asleep, having just returned from a weekend in the country, with all its stimulations.

The conversation turns to Stanley and Sophie. "Your dogs, so different from each other," Richard says. He describes how Stanley comes right up to his front door demanding to be let in so he can investigate.

I defend Sophie. "She's usually all piss and vinegar. Not like this at all." I don't share my thoughts about the Transylvanian ambience, although Richard would more likely be amused than offended.

"You chose good parents. James—a loving man. Very kind. Sigrid and Desmond—perfect for a dog like Stanley. Strong people."

"Dumb luck," I say.

"Good instincts," he says.

As it happens, Sigrid and Richard have forged a special

bond. They've discovered that they were both refugees from the same part of Germany, Mecklenburg, fleeing as children with their families from the advance of the Soviet army at the end of World War II. Sigrid marvels at the circularity of life; I marvel at the skeins of friendship formed around dogs.

Richard understands why I gave up the dogs and thinks they are much the better for it, but he asks me how I'm feeling, whether I have regrets. "The other day," I tell him, "I had a moment when I wanted *everything* back. Not just the dogs. The apartment, the books, the furniture, the whole shebang. If only I'd had the money. If only . . ." I stop myself. "I also wanted my husband raised from the dead. I was feeling *very* sorry for myself. *Disgustingly* sorry. But I suppose that's allowed now and again, like once every fifty years." He laughs.

As Richard nears the end of the stripping process, we come to a critical decision. How big should Sophie's mustache be? As with weight, the size of whiskers for borders has been a subject of vigorous debate. I prefer a small mustache because a big one gets crusty from food, such as yogurt grubbed out of the bottom of containers, something both Stanley and Sophie love to do; Richard prefers a larger one. I tell Richard the story about a meeting before World War I when a show-dog type tried to make a mustache a part of the breed standard, arguing that the better ones always seemed to sport one. An indignant farmer scotched *that* suggestion: "Aye. And do you know what will happen? In less than three years' time you will have something like the bloody German emperor back in your blasted show rings."

Today Sophie leaves with a small mustache. Out on the

street, she shakes off her resentment about the stripping session and, without hesitating, turns left and beetles along the sidewalk with a determination that won't be brooked. That's the direction to Charles Street, to James and Christopher. Enough with grandmothers.

9.

Rolling Pin

Stanley and Sophie are the luckiest of dogs, blessed with heapings of variety, lashings of love. "Sophie has a whole village raising her," says James, who is as sociable as I am solitary and has an extensive circle of friends. At Pantai Berawa, my brother tells me, Chico and Cheeky were moved into enormous cages that Salim built for them to my specifications, and a real village is raising them. My brother also tells me that a third monkey, Gigi, has been added to the family. She's a baby, the same size as Cheeky when she came to Puri Angsa but a much happier monkey because she has Cheeky, who has elected herself Gigi's teacher and protector. Although she's not much bigger than a baby herself, Cheeky shields Gigi, placing her valiant self between her charge and the world. If Chico approaches Gigi, Cheeky chases him away, roundly berating him, boxing his ears; all that's missing is a rolling pin. Sister, mother, aunt all in one. May the rain fall soft on her.

10.

A Gentle Spring Day

For the longest time, the ferocity of my love for the dogs, its depth, its completeness, baffled me. I knew I was compensating for the loss of my husband; that much was obvious. What didn't occur to me was that my role in my dogs' lives was the same as the one I had played in my husband's as he vanished into the grotesque infancy of Alzheimer's. I was his interlocutor, interpreting his wishes, speaking for him. I coaxed and cajoled, swaddled him in love. I defended and translated. When Stanley arrived, I took up where I'd left off when my husband died; it came easy.

I also betrayed them both. I made decisions, for the best, through love. I placed my husband in a nursing home toward the end of his illness. When he walked into the lobby of the home and realized where he was and what was happening, he howled his betrayal, his disbelieving hurt, just like Stanley in the park: "You!" My husband forgot my betrayal, as he forgot everything; his story could have no happy ending. What Stanley recollects, what goes on in his noggin, who knows? But recollect he undoubtedly does, with an accuracy that can be astounding. Sometimes I think he has forgiven me, sometimes not. My imagination, maybe. My father thinks that nothing escapes dogs; they are watchful and knowing, our equals; they understand. And in their way, they remember.

Here's a moment that's stayed with me. It's late on a gentle spring day. Sigrid, Stanley, and I have been down to the Hudson, climbed back up the steep stairs to Riverside Park, stopped to check out who's in the dog run. We've communed a moment with the statue of Eleanor Roosevelt—greathearted Eleanor—said our goodbyes, and now Sigrid and Stanley are headed home along Riverside Drive to Desmond, to dinner, tall woman and small dog, small dog compensating for his size with his purposeful walk, almost a strut, like a miniature football player. Rugby, not gridiron. Stanley doesn't look back at me watching them. No need for that. And I can make as much or as little of the fishhooks in my heart as I'm inclined.

New Dispatches from the (Extended) Families of Stanley and Sophie

Sophie

James Lecesne

How many times have I had to sit while some dear friend recounted the litany of extraordinary feats that their turtle can do on command? How many photographs of cats have I had to examine, hoping to see the signs of intelligence and cuteness that their owners claim to be evident? How many dogs have I watched sit and speak? Don't even get me started on the virtues of the llamas I've known. It gets tiring. So naturally, I'm more than a little hesitant to discuss the virtues of my dog, Sophie, with strangers.

She is, of course, a genius.

But she didn't come to me that way. In fact, she arrived slightly traumatized from living too long with a very alpha-male terrier named Stanley. Sophie wasn't house-trained when I got her. She was a shaggy-coated, grizzle and tan border terrier prone to gnawing her back leg until the fur was worn away, and overly fond of running in circles. She wasn't eating that much because Stanley hadn't allowed her a fair share. And she didn't know "sit" from "come."

At the time, I was living in a big downtown loft on Greene

Street, and I remember Sophie as a wild ball of fur whizzing and whirling from one end of the place to the other. And when I say whizzing, I mean peeing. After having lived in apartments for the first couple of years of her life she must have felt as though she had free reign at this Valhalla. But even Valhalla has rules, and together we set about to learn them.

As with all dogs, there were plenty of wrong turns. Many of those mistakes were memorialized into the white carpet that my boyfriend and I had foolishly purchased shortly before Sophie came on the scene. But eventually, the carpet was removed, and she began to see the advantages of living according to the rules.

Some of them.

If you've ever known a border terrier, you know the breed possesses independence, a trait that is constantly at war with their strong desire to please. Border terriers don't take kindly to every rule. It's pick and choose, according to their whim. They are cats in dog suits, pretending to be man's best friend while in fact entertaining an agenda of their own. Personally, I'm all for any creature that holds itself in high regard and considers itself a creature not just of habit but of principle. And Sophie is just that. From underneath that shaking bit of fur and snarl, a charming little princess of a dog emerged, one perfectly polite to strangers but intolerant of other dogs that might steal her thunder.

These days, Sophie has an ideal life trotting around the West Village and occasionally visiting various downtown dog runs. She summers in Provincetown, where she can roam mostly free along the beaches, and has proved an agreeable traveling companion, allowing herself to go limp in a bag and be stuffed under an airline seat. Anything for an adventure. But perhaps the most surprising aspect of my life with Sophie is that she came with Kate Jennings. The one thing that kept me from owning a dog was that I wouldn't be able to take care of it. What if I had to go out of town? Not only is Kate more than willing to spend the occasional week with her fur girl, but she has also become an excellent grandmother to Sophie, spoiling her to death and seeing her back to health when, as happened this past summer, she contracted a fierce fungus from some other dog at the run. This is a two-for-one deal, a dog's life that both Kate and I could never have imagined for ourselves. It took Sophie to do it for us.

Sophie's genius is being herself. She exudes an *is-ness* unlike any other dog I've ever known. She doesn't reflect me back to myself; she's not a creature dependent on my mood and movements. She speaks her own language, and she has taught it to me slowly and over time. In fact, I sometimes think that it is she who trained me, taught me to be more patient, to have a little fun, to let go and run down the street just because, to stop and smell whatever, to sit and speak. And she did this by simply coming into my life and being herself. Genius.

Stanley

SIGRID MACRAE

The story of how Stanley came into our life is pure New York: lives crisscrossing, touching, if only tangentially, in ever-widening circles until . . . bing! A new family is created.

Dreary March weather. Daughter gone to California; old dog gone to the happy hunting ground. Gloom. Desmond tosses a flyer on my desk, an email about a border terrier looking for a home. It was sent to someone at the *New York Times,* who passed it to a neighbor, also at the *Times,* who already has a dog and passed it on to a friend, who walks lots of local dogs and is partial to borders.

Dated 9:57 A.M, February 22, 2005, it's a crummy, black-and-white computer printout of a small dog sitting on a table next to a pot of what must be bright daffodils, but appear as a gray blur. Scrawled across the bottom: "Joyce" and an arrow pointing up, "Stanley—(Can you be tempted?)." The attached sheet describes a purebred border needing a new home "due to circumstances beyond his owner's control." He is "accommodating, gentlemanly, with impeccable manners, sensitive, affectionate. . . . Just look at his eyes—they say it all." Indeed.

He looks straight into the camera, his whole body taut with wishing he weren't on that table, big dark eyes conveying a quiet but unmistakable feel of what-you-see-is-what-I-am. I can be tempted.

A flurry of emails and phone calls leads to a meeting on neutral turf: the Central Park boat basin, where a gaggle of bundled-up folks with telescopes keep watch over Lola and Pale Male, the red-tailed hawks nesting on Fifth Avenue. We recognize Kate because we recognize Stanley. Formalities accomplished, Stanley gets to demonstrate his inimitable style on a joint walk, trotting jauntily along the granite edge of the boat basin, then sniffing exhaustively at almost everything on the path. Suddenly he hurls his body and a barrage of furious barks at a big Lab ambling by.

What's this? Impeccable manners? Well, an issue with Labs—part of his style—we learn. Yet he sits patiently through coffee at Bethesda Fountain, where our conversation rambles across books, writing, finance, and a difficult crossroads in Kate's life. Stanley moves onto Desmond's lap to give his ear a quick lick. We've been vetted; we mesh.

We're in love.

More walks, coffee, talk, emails. We become part of one another's lives. On one outing, I have Stanley's leash when Kate unexpectedly thrusts a folder under my arm—his papers. "He's yours," she says. "If you want him, take him." She turns and walks away. Stanley lets out a single heartbreaking wail. It's a bad moment. We rush him away, and soon he's sniffing at dead leaves, undergrowth, lampposts.

It took time for him to make eye contact. He's a tender soul, but he's got his dignity; he's not a pushover. It took time for Kate to feel ready to see him again, too. Two hearts had fractured. With Kate far away, I email news of Stanley; she emails exotica from down under and Bali. She returns to an ecstatic reunion. We share books, birthdays, french fries with Stanley at the café by the river. We visit in the park and at the hospital, edit each other, commiserate, water each other's plants.

When we got Stanley, we got a package: Stanley, Kate, Irene, Sophie, and James, too. When Irene dognaps him for the weekend, he is frantic with joy. She is, after all, we've reluctantly agreed, the love of his life. Now, once we get to Seventy-second Street, he knows where we're headed. Sniffing abates; the pace picks up. Dog on a mission: make a right at Sixty-sixth, wow the doormen, fly straight to the elevators, down the hall to Kate, backlit by bright windows, waiting in her doorway. Two hearts have mended. We are a new, ad hoc New York family, knitted together not by birth or genes, but by common interests, affection, and a dog who loves us all.

INTRODUCTION

"I fell in love with a prideful, tense bundle of muscle and sinew that stood seventeen inches high. You would see a small brown dog; I saw perfection."

So begins the story of Kate Jennings's unexpected love affair with two border terriers: first Stanley, then a few years later, Sophie. A fiercely intelligent writer, an astute observer of people and her surroundings, a recent widow now ready to face her grief, an irascible Australian with no time for indulgent New Yorkers and their pampered pets, Jennings falls hard. She is swept off her feet, stunned by the depth of her love. Her life is suddenly overtaken by Stanley, and when she is seduced into getting a companion for him, by the pair of them.

But after several years with her willful yet cherished dogs, Jennings came to the heartrending realization that they needed more than she could give—and that she must reassess her own life, too. First and foremost, *Stanley and Sophie* is a book about dogs, understanding them and doing the best by them. It is also a vivid chronicle of Jennings's grief and sadness—for the loss of a husband, for the city after September 11, for two pigtailed macaques in Bali, for a world going to hell in a handbasket. This is a bittersweet and darkly humorous memoir about the way two demanding, idiosyncratic, exhilarating dogs gave Jennings daily purpose and showed her the way to her own heart.

Discussion

1. In *Stanley and Sophie,* Kate Jennings describes having fallen in love at first sight only twice in her life—both times with dogs. What is it about dogs that allows for this kind of infatuation and emotional immediacy? How does the author's love for Stanley and Sophie relate to her own heightened sense of need? How is her love story entwined with her feelings about Manhattan, and how might those feelings also be described in terms of love?

2. "Who can stay sad around a creature so evidently bent on discovery, so palpably pleased to be in this world?" (page 19). What is it about Stanley's personality that enables the author to transcend her own sadness and sense of loss? What do Stanley's special qualities as a border terrier have to do with the author's total immersion in his world? To what extent does her absorption with Stanley seem akin to a love affair?

3. What does the author's research into the history and temperament of the border terrier breed reveal about her own interest in Stanley's exemplifying the "best of the breed"? Why did she gravitate toward the terrier breed in the first place? How would you characterize border terriers, based on the author's detailed descriptions?

4. "New York City is a moody city, transmitting emotions as if it were an organic being" (page 53). How does the author's perspective of life in New York City change in the aftermath of the September 11 attacks? What role does Stanley play in her ability to process the tragedy? How might a nonnative be able to interpret New York and its moods with greater objectivity than a native New Yorker?

5. "How on earth did this happen? How did it come about that I was spending my days adjudicating between two dogs who

were acting out the story of my life?" (page 69). What compels the author to adopt a second border terrier? How do Stanley and Sophie's responses to each other reveal their individual natures? Why does the author feel her dogs are repeating her own life in their canine dramas?

6. How does her identity as a dog owner come to shape the author? How does her role as parent to Stanley and Sophie transform her life in New York? To what extent does owning dogs enable the author to make deeper friendships and connections with people? How does her own attitude toward dogs change once she adopts Stanley?

7. "I inched toward a resolution that would have been inconceivable even a month before: to dismantle my life, to change it radically, beginning with Stanley and Sophie" (page 84). What prompts the author to consider giving away her dogs to new families? Were you surprised by this decision? What might giving the dogs away represent for the author?

8. How do the author's experiences in Indonesia heighten her appreciation of the economic, environmental, and social challenges faced by that country? In what respects does her attachment to the resident macaques at Puri Angsa, Chico and Cheeky, seem like an extension of her love for Stanley and Sophie? What ironies do you see in her returning to New York to escape from the terrorism in Bali?

9. "What Stanley recollects, what goes on in his noggin, who knows? But recollect he undoubtedly does, with an accuracy that can be astounding" (page 175). How does the author's depiction of Stanley and Sophie offer a glimpse into the interior world of the border terrier? What aspects of her dogs' personalities does the author seem to have an especially keen and instinctive understanding of? To what extent are these dogs like human beings? Of the many anecdotes about Stanley and Sophie in this memoir, which were most memorable to you and why?

Enhance Your Book Club

1. As border terriers—dogs renowned for their athleticism, independence, and sociability—Stanley and Sophie embody the best of their breed. Do you currently own a border terrier, or could you be interested in adopting one? You may want to visit the Border Terrier Club of America's extremely thorough website: http://www.btcoa.org/. There you can find extensive information about border terrier current events, clubs in your region, a photo gallery, and relevant publications regarding border terriers as a breed. Might there be a Stanley or Sophie in your future?

2. Kate Jennings's deep love for Stanley and Sophie enables her to come to terms with her grief in both the aftermath of her husband's death and the September 11 tragedy that befalls her adopted city. Have you ever found yourself depending on a cherished pet or a loved one to help you cope with a difficult time in your life? Think of some of the challenges you've faced and recall who came to your aid. If you've been fortunate enough never to have experienced a troubled period in your life, who would you depend on in a time of need? How might a loved pet help?

3. Would you ever consider visiting Indonesia, the country Kate Jennings visits in *Stanley and Sophie*? Whether you are just intrigued by this amazing archipelago of some seventeen thousand islands or you are planning an actual trip, you will want to visit the CIA's comprehensive dossier on the country at https://www.cia.gov/library/publications/the-world-factbook/geos/id.html. Here you can read about Indonesia's people, its government, its economy, and some of the transnational issues that it faces.

About the Author

KATE JENNINGS, a poet, essayist, and novelist, grew up in the Australian Outback. She attended the University of Sydney in the late 1960s, where she gained notoriety as a feminist activist. She moved to New York City in 1979. Her novel *Snake* was a *New York Times* Notable Book of the Year, as was *Moral Hazard*, which was based on her experiences as a Wall Street speechwriter. Her work has been in contention for the Booker, IMPAC, and *Los Angeles Times* literary prizes. In her native country, she has won the prestigious Christina Stead and Adelaide Festival prizes and was honored with the Australian Literature Society Gold Medal.